M000318085

YOUR

CEO

POTENTIAL

YOUR

CEO

POTENTIAL

REALIZING YOUR
CALLING, EQUIPPING, AND OUTCOMES
IN CHRIST JESUS

KAMAL I. LATHAM

Your CEO Potential: Realizing Your Calling, Equipping, and Outcomes in Christ Jesus
Copyright © 2020 by Kamal I. Latham

Published by Kamal I. Latham

All rights reserved. No part of this publication may be reproduced, stored in a retrieval system, or transmitted in any form or by any means, electronic, mechanical, photocopying, recording, or otherwise, except for brief quotations in reviews, without the prior written permission of the publisher.

Kamal I. Latham titles may be purchased in bulk for educational, business, fundraising, or sales promotional use. For information, please email Info@KamalLatham.com

ISBN 978-1-7347001-2-1 (paperback)
ISBN 978-1-7347001-1-4 (hardcover)
ISBN 978-1-7347001-0-7 (ebook)

Scripture taken from the New King James Version®.
Copyright © 1982 by Thomas Nelson.
Used by permission. All rights reserved.

Scripture quotations taken from the Amplified® Bible (AMP),
Copyright © 2015 by The Lockman Foundation.
Used by permission. www.Lockman.org

Scripture quotations taken from the Amplified® Bible (AMPC),
Copyright © 1954, 1958, 1962, 1964, 1965, 1987 by The Lockman Foundation.
Used by permission. www.Lockman.org

Scripture quotations marked (NLT) are taken from the Holy Bible, New Living Translation, copyright ©1996, 2004, 2015 by Tyndale House Foundation. Used by permission of Tyndale House Publishers, a Division of Tyndale House Ministries, Carol Stream, Illinois 60188. All rights reserved.

Any internet addresses (websites, blogs, etc.) in this book are offered as a resource. They are not intended in any way to be or imply an endorsement by Kamal I. Latham, nor does Kamal I. Latham vouch for the content of these sites for the life of this book.

Cover design: Ma'at "Yani" Latham
Cover photo: Alexandra Querrard
Interior design: Melinda Martin

Actual life events featured in this work are presented as accurately as possible based upon the recollection of the author. Some dialogue has been modified and events compressed to respect privacy.

DEDICATION

In loving memory of my mother, Pamela E. Edwards,
who urged me to not forget John 3:16.

CONTENTS

ACKNOWLEDGMENTS

I thank my lovely wife Jonnel, son Micah, and daughter Nasyra for their continuous love and unwavering support, especially when I was acting unlovely and unsupportive.

I thank my editors Karen Engle and Crystal Ladwig who were instrumental in refining and clarifying the message God gave me to deliver.

INTRODUCTION

One evening many years ago, my mother told me to not forget John 3:16. Although I was already a Christian and knew the Scripture, I had no idea until later in life that it contained the key to realizing my calling, equipping, and outcomes potential in Christ Jesus. Implementing two simple actions embedded within this Scripture activated my faith, without which I could not please God and release His power in my life.

In the New King James Version of the Bible, John 3:16 reads as follows: "For God so loved the world that He gave His only begotten Son, that whoever believes in Him should not perish but have everlasting life" (NKJV). God performed two actions: He loved and gave. He loved the world so much that He gave it the most valuable thing to Him, His only Son Jesus Christ. You are called to love God and give Him your most valuable asset, too: your own life.

Surrender to God, and the following three things will happen: 1) You will understand your calling; 2) You will receive the equipping needed to carry out your calling; and 3) You will have successful outcomes. Many Christians are saved by Jesus but are not *led* by Jesus. "Surrendering" to God means accepting Jesus Christ as both *Savior* and *Lord*. Many people confess Jesus with their mouth, believe in Him with their heart, and declare they are saved. However, they ignore Jesus' teachings and do not walk in love. When Christians say Jesus is Savior but live as if He is not Lord, they are destined to die without fulfilling their calling. They have not surrendered their life to Him.

When your love for God compels you to surrender your life to Him, you will be in a prime position to understand your purpose for living. Additionally, you will be able to comprehend how to tap into the talents you possess. You were born to do something specific and unique. God placed and shaped you in your mother's womb and gave you His Holy Spirit and Holy Word. Regardless of where you were born or how you were raised, God is ready to fulfill His will for your life. It is impossible for you to fail unless you choose to fail.

Do not be like Adam and Eve, the first people written about in the book of Genesis. They were called and equipped to dominate the earth but failed due to disobedience. God formed them from the dust of the earth and breathed into them the breath of life, which was His Holy Spirit. Afterward, God gave them His Holy Word when He blessed them and told them to be fruitful, multiply, and rule the earth. Since God is holy, the spirit He breathed into them was His Holy Spirit, and the words He spoke to them were His Holy Word.

Despite all this holiness, Eve chose to be deceived by a talking serpent and followed her lustful desire for worldly wisdom. She ate fruit from the tree of the knowledge of good and evil and disobeyed

God. Adam chose to listen to his wife Eve when she offered him the same tainted fruit. He also ate it and disobeyed God. Both were punished and kicked out of the garden of Eden. Who you obey is who you serve. Adam and Eve made the serpent their master when they did his bidding and ate the forbidden fruit. Because of their actions, they handed over their God-given mantle of leadership to the enemy. They could no longer rule and reign over the earth. That power now belonged to the serpent. This was a failed outcome.

What was the big deal about eating fruit from a particular tree? Father God, Jesus Christ, and the Holy Spirit made Adam and Eve in their likeness and image and put them in the garden of Eden. God made every tree grow in the garden that looked attractive and produced good food. The tree of life and the tree of the knowledge of good and evil were also present. God told Adam and Eve they could freely eat from any tree except the tree of the knowledge of good and evil. God was not obligated to explain Himself, but they were called to follow His will. The pair committed sin by disobeying God and eating the forbidden fruit. Death was the penalty for their actions. Sadly, the couple loved themselves more than God and gave their lives to the serpent.

The Adam and Eve situation raises an important question. If the first people in the Bible got it wrong, then who can get it right? The answer is simple: whoever loves God and gives their life to Him. Doing these two basic things—loving God and giving your life to Him—will activate your faith and make you righteous. Without faith, it is impossible to please God (Hebrews 11:6) and release His power in your life.

God calls every Christian to do something spectacular. Every Christian is equipped with the Holy Spirit and the Word of God to do the impossible. Every Christian is destined to see outstanding outcomes in every aspect of their life. However, every Christian must walk by faith and put their trust in the power of God to realize their calling, equipping, and outcomes potential in Christ Jesus.

Fortunately, the Bible is full of stories of people who got it right—a pioneer, a brother, a visionary, and a spokesperson all activated their faith and did great things. This does not mean they were without sin; rather, they chose to please God. Sometimes their decision to follow God resulted in difficult or demanding situations. Despite the circumstance, each person rose to the occasion and fulfilled their purpose.

This book was written for people who want to discover their purpose, develop their God-given gift, and deliver God-pleasing results. I am a Christian and knew God called me to do great things and gave me His Holy Spirit and Holy Word to make it happen. However, I did not see victorious outcomes on a consistent basis. My faith walk seemed to be hit and miss with more misses than hits. I felt like I was living beneath my potential and disappointing God.

Do you find yourself in the same boat? Do you feel powerless to change your situation? Do you feel like you are not pleasing God? Do you want to break down the walls around you? Do you want to break out of a mediocre life? Do you want to walk in joy and peace? Do you want to walk in power and dominion? If you are a Christian and answered yes to any of these questions, then this book was also written for you. However, if you answered no to these questions, then this book may be for a Christian in your life who is struggling and needs help.

Okay, I know you might be excited about getting your life back on track but are questioning whether you can overcome your fear, self-doubt, and laziness. You may have tried and failed to walk by faith in the past. You might not be sure what you could do different this time to honor and obey your God. You may have confessed Christ as your Savior but have not made Him your Lord. You might have said you loved God but have not given Him your life.

My hope is that what is shared in this book will help open your eyes, turn on the lights, and show you God's power. The first topic discussed will be finding your calling, receiving your equipping, and realizing your outcomes, with insights from my life mixed in. Then, how deception destroys potential and how faith realizes potential will be examined. Finally, how faith releases power will be discussed. Profiles of nine different calling types will follow. Afterward, the faith journey of Noah, Joseph, John the Baptist, Paul the Apostle, and other great people in the Bible will be traced to reveal how God called and equipped them to succeed. Lastly, the victory move you need to make today will be reviewed: walk in love. This book could put you on the path to reveal, reinvigorate, or resurrect your calling.

However, you'll be responsible for applying the principles and walking by faith. No one else can do that for you. What you do—or do not do—will determine whether you succeed or fail. Faith is required to please God and release His power. The two keys to activating your faith, which works by love, are loving God and giving Him your life.

After reading and putting into practice the principles in this book, you can expect the power of God manifested in your life. The power to love, the power to give, the power to heal, the power to forgive, and more, will flow out of you. You will lead yourself, your family, your team, your organization, your ministry, your business, your platoon, your agency, or your country with clarity and confidence. You will fulfill your calling and enjoy your life.

What are you waiting for? Start the journey.

— Kamal I. Latham

CHAPTER 1

CALLING, EQUIPPING, AND OUTCOMES

FIND YOUR CALLING

What is your calling? What are you called to do? What are you called to be? I have asked myself these questions time and time again. Often, I thought I had it figured out—only to be proven wrong. It has taken me years to fully understand why I was conceived. Life is no fun when you do not know (or are confused about) why you were created. You need to know why you were separated from your mother's womb. You need to know the purpose of the breath in your lungs. You need to know the reason for your existence. You need to know your calling.

Everything about *you* is an intentional, preordained, and perfect plan of God. This is not to be confused with everything you *do* because what you *do* might not reflect the real *you*. The real *you* that you need to know is the person created and called to fulfill a charge in this world. There is an amazing God-inspired purpose for your life that awaits your discovery. Finding it will be satisfying to your soul. God sacrificed His one and only Son for you because He loves you and wants you to have abundant life.

But what kind of life are you leading right now? Are you happy with your current state of affairs or sad about where you are today? What is your spiritual, emotional, physical, relational, and financial condition? Are you heading into a ditch or stepping into your destiny? Decisions you make every day shape your present and future. Like an umpire, you need to make good calls, not bad calls. Life is not a game, but you must train hard and play well if you want to win. How can you maximize your performance and end a losing streak? Learn under the best coach in the business of life, Jesus. Coach Christ will show you how to play and dominate.

> Decisions you make every day shape your present and future.

Every athlete knows they need a purpose, a plan, and power to perform. Regardless of whether it is an individual or team sport, players planning to win need a clear aim, a specific strategy, and solid effort. Life is no different. You need a stated goal, a process to achieve it, and the wherewithal to reach it. This might sound simple, but so does taking a stick and hitting a ball with it. The complexity lies in consistently swinging and hitting the ball at the right spot, at the right angle, and at the right time. Success in sports—and in life—boils down to two core skills: consistency and accuracy.

Consistency and accuracy come with faithfulness and persistence. A faithful person is reliable, dependable, and predictable. A persistent person is dedicated, determined, and driven. Faithful and persistent people think the right thoughts, say the right words, and do the right things. They control their emotions rather than being emotional.

They exercise self-control rather than being selfish. They show love to everyone rather than being selective. These people have the patience, integrity, and character to propel themselves into their happy place—again and again and again. Their reputation is solid, and their success is evident.

Follow Jesus and you'll find your calling. Find your calling and you'll find your happy place. Find your happy place and you'll find fulfillment in life. It is that simple. Jesus Christ enables you to access Father God through the Holy Spirit. You need Father God, Jesus Christ, and the Holy Spirit. They are three entities operating as one. Do you know your purpose for living? Have you seen the game plan for your life? Do you have the power to succeed? Father God has your purpose, Jesus Christ has your plan, and the Holy Spirit is your power.

Father God has called you to do great things with your life and equipped you with His Holy Word and His Holy Spirit to make it happen. Failure is not an option when you are doing what Scripture says and walking in the power and authority of God. How do you find *and* fulfill your calling in Christ Jesus? Invest quality time with God daily. How much time should you allocate? Enough time to develop an intimate relationship.

A great way to achieve intimacy is to tithe your time to God. Aside from your lifeblood, time is your most valuable asset. Tithing time to the Lord may involve praise, worship, prayer, meditation, Bible study, and listening to His voice—all roads leading to Him. When you commune with the Lord, knowledge, wisdom, and revelation will flow from Him. You will learn your calling in Christ Jesus and receive power from the Holy Spirit to achieve it. Great outcomes will testify of the glory of God in your life.

WHAT YOU ARE CALLED TO *DO*

You have a God-given calling on your life. It is the reason you live. There are different types of callings, and one has your name next to it.

> You have a God-given calling on your life.

However, before moving down the discovery path, let us first distinguish between what you are called to *do* and what you are called to *be*. What you are called to *do* is your permanent position, while what you are called to *be* is your temporary condition. Understand the difference and you will better understand yourself.

What you are called to *do* is who you are and spans your entire life. This is your spiritual profile that influences your natural lifestyle. Think of it as your permanent position. It does not change. It does not evolve. It remains the same. What you are called to *do* cuts across every aspect and dynamic of your life. You cannot run, escape, or hide from it. You cannot experience true happiness, joy, or peace without doing it. You cannot effectively relate to the world around you apart from it. What you are called to *do* is your life mark. It is present with you right now and will be with you when you die. It shapes your personality and impacts your relationships. It is the legacy you will leave behind.

To illustrate this point, I will use myself as an example. I am called to inspire. Specifically, I am called to inspire people to believe in a better tomorrow. Preaching and teaching the Word of God are the most impactful things I have ever done to inspire men, women, and children. When I die, I hope many lives will have been positively impacted because of my life. Perhaps someone listening at my homegoing service will be inspired to love their neighbor more than they did the day before and be a greater blessing. What we do to others is what matters most. The words I want to hear after I exit this world are "well done My good and faithful servant, enter into My rest" (Matthew 25:23). Fulfilling my God-given calling with the love of Christ in my heart will best position me to receive what I desire from my Lord and Savior.

During my life, the best professional and volunteer assignments I had were when I was able to inspire others through my work or actions. Whether that was through better public policy, better economic opportunities, or better leadership, I thrived in environments where my natural talents and skills advanced hope for a better tomorrow. This doesn't mean every endeavor I engaged in was successful—I've had my share of failures and missteps (more than I would care to have had). But every experience shaped and sharpened my soul.

WHAT YOU ARE CALLED TO *BE*

What you are called to *be* is a result of what you are called to *do*. This is your specific assignment, task, or job, which could be a responsibility, passion, or occupation. This is what you are busy with during a particular season. This is your realm of personal and/or professional passion. You feel strongly about what you are to *be*. You stay awake some nights addressing it. Although it is God-ordained, think of it as your temporary condition. "Temporary" in this context means you are not engaged in this activity from cradle to grave (although it could last decades). It may change. It may evolve. It might not remain the same. What you are called to *be* does not necessarily infuse throughout your entire life. You could lose a taste for it and walk away. You could complete the task and move on. You could be quite successful but disconnect due to resignation or retirement.

Finding out what you are called to *be* is not necessarily a complicated and mysterious phenomenon requiring forty days and nights of fasting. However, it may require spending quality time with God. What you are called to *be* is important. It might be the way you make a living and provide for you or your family. However, it flows from what you are called to *do*, which is the emphasis of this book. Knowing what you are called to *do* will clarify what you are called to *be*. Understanding what to *do* will reveal where to invest time and energy.

> Knowing what you are called to *do* will clarify what you are called to *be*.

My big mistake was focusing more on what I was called to *be* during a particular season of my life and not on what I was called to *do* throughout my life.

MY STORY

So, who am I? I am a blessed man who grew up in America encompassed by love. On January 24, 1974, I was born to a beautiful native New Yorker named Pamela E. Edwards and a handsome man from the nation of Panama, Aristides Latham. My mother raised me in Queens, New York, and loved me dearly. She was a strong, no-nonsense black woman who reared me, worked hard, and believed in the Lord. She sacrificed for me to have an excellent education and the best opportunities to succeed in life. I was her parents' first grandchild and was doted upon heavily. My maternal grandparents, aunts, uncles, and cousins showered love upon me. I was a blessed child.

My grandfather, Marion P. Edwards Jr., was a World War II veteran and spent his career in the telecommunications industry. I looked up to him and remember how he provided for the family. Edna M. Edwards, my dear grandmother, was a devout Christian who prayed regularly. She diligently served believers through a Baptist church and was the reason why some family members even went to church. She was a humble saint who loved Jesus. As a child, I heard about God from "granny."

This is a photo of me in my maternal grandparents' home
(c. late 1970s).

Although my story might not be your story, some of my life lessons might be helpful. I decided to give my life to Jesus as a teenager. God sent a godly man across my path and used him to minister the gospel to me in junior high school. During Resurrection Sunday in 1989, I accepted the salvation invitation and gave my life to Christ. God used my family to sow godliness into my heart and worked through a godly man to water the seed. My mom, Pamela, encouraged my faith in God when she fervently urged me to never forgot John 3:16 and reminded me that God loved the world so much that He gave His only begotten Son Jesus to die for it. The memory of my mom telling me with intense eyes to never forget what God did through Christ is seared into my consciousness.

COUNSEL FOR YOUR CALLING

Seek God and His kingdom first and everything else in your life will fall into place. Closeness with the Lord will open your heart to receive divine instruction and guidance. Life will be challenging, and there will be many voices seeking to influence your thoughts, words, and deeds. If you think you know what you are called to *do* or called to *be*, you would be well advised to gain knowledge, wisdom, and understanding in those areas. God can counsel you through His Holy Spirit or through His Holy Word. He can even get His message across through other people (such as a spouse or pastor) or

> Seek God and His kingdom first and everything else in your life will fall into place.

via personal, academic, and professional experiences. The bottom line is: seek counsel, and be open to receive it.

In 1992, I enrolled in Temple University. I completed several internships in Washington, DC and met an array of leaders. My undergraduate academic career at Temple culminated in a Bachelor of Arts Degree. I double majored in Political Science and History and minored in East Asian Studies. Realizing the importance of financial markets, I thought it would be a good idea to work on Wall Street. I landed a job as a financial analyst with a bulge-bracket investment bank. It was a great experience, but I was not passionate about doing that for my entire career. After finishing my assignment, I pursued my dream of obtaining a Master of Public Policy degree from the John F. Kennedy School of Government at Harvard University.

ENVISION YOUR CALLING

You might be totally clueless—or fully confident—about what you are called to *do* or called to *be*. Regardless of what end of the spectrum you are on, you must see yourself doing or being something of value. You have worth and importance because you are created in the image and likeness of God. It is important to see yourself moving down the road God paved for you. Visualizing your future

> You have worth and importance because you are created in the image and likeness of God.

will help you see challenges and prepare solutions in advance. People who plan for the future have a strategic advantage over those who do not. Without vision people perish (Proverbs 29:18). Jesus must have envisioned Himself being crucified on the cross because He spoke about it multiple times beforehand and prayed several times in Gethsemane to Father God leading up to it. Seeing Himself fulfilling the will of God must have helped Him go through it.

Who do you see when you look into a mirror? Do you see a success or a failure? What you see is what you will have. Change the view of yourself if it does not line up with the Word of God. God said through His Word that you are blessed and favored. You have the power of the Almighty God dwelling within you and everything He called you to do will come to pass. Do not fear, but believe. Simple childlike faith in the King of Glory will resolve the issues in your blessed life. God provides for all His people. His vision is for you to prosper. Trust Him with all your heart by putting your faith in Him. He will never leave you nor forsake you. Father God bought you with the blood of His Son Jesus, which makes you His prized possession. There is nothing you can do to separate yourself from His love. Just believe.

ADVANCE YOUR CALLING

Do you have any inkling of why you were put on the earth? Breathing is good but insufficient to fulfill the will of God unless you are supposed to be dead and your breath is a miracle. There must be something you like doing. Be creative and find worthwhile projects you can work on and activities you can engage in to add value to others. Serving people is a great way to stir up gifts you possess. People matter to God, and the more you do for others, the more God will do for you. Do not be concerned about what you will reap if you sow good seeds. Have a strategy and work it. Successful farmers are intentional in what they plant. Have a growth plan. Establish

> Harness the winds, weather the storms, and keep moving forward. God is with you.

goals and develop winning strategies. Even if you are off base, you can always course correct. It is impossible to finish what is not started. Chart a course and set sail. Harness the winds, weather the storms, and keep moving forward. God is with you.

RECEIVE YOUR EQUIPPING

How has God equipped you to carry out His will and purpose? He has given you His Holy Spirit and Holy Word. You are empowered to carry what you were designed to handle. His Spirit and Word are all you need to perform assigned tasks in the fullness of decency and order. The breath of God residing

> Receive the Spirit and the Word into your heart and be equipped to reach your full potential in Christ Jesus.

within your lungs is the manifestation of the Holy Spirit. Without the Holy Spirit, you cannot live. The wisdom of God revealed within your spirit is the manifestation of the Word of God. Without the Word, you cannot prosper. Receive the Spirit and the Word into your heart and be equipped to reach your full potential in Christ Jesus.

The Holy Spirit within you is a seed to be nurtured and grown. A tree of righteousness awaits those who invest time and energy into developing their spirit of faith, which is the Holy Spirit. Hearing the

Word of God builds your spirit of faith because faith comes by hearing the Word of God. Read the Bible aloud to yourself. Listen to audio recordings of the Bible. Listen to anointed and Spirit-filled ministers preach and teach the Word. Listen to praise and worship music glorifying God. Surround yourself with people who love the Lord and speak the Word. You will be positively impacted by these influences and grow in godly wisdom. People will recognize the call of God upon you and give you opportunities to walk in your purpose.

On September 1, 2001, Jonnel and I married. It was a beautiful sunny day in Atlanta, Georgia. Our regal mothers, many family members, and friends came to witness our vows and celebrate. Our wedding was a blessed and joyous occasion.

Wedding picture of Jonnel and I,
September 1, 2001.

Jonnel on our wedding day.

Here I am pictured with my mom
during my wedding.

Ten days after Jonnel and I married, airplanes flew into the Twin Towers of the World Trade Center in New York City, and the whole world changed. By November of that same year, Jonnel and I were both dispatched to Shenyang, China—a remote industrial city in Northeast China nestled between Russia and North Korea—to represent America as diplomats. After graduating from Harvard, I launched a promising career as a US Foreign Service Officer. My appointment as a diplomat was from the highest official in government, the then-sitting president of the United States, George W. Bush.

Jonnel and I were saved and Spirit-filled Christians who believed in Father God, Jesus Christ, and the Holy Spirit. We were "churched" in non-denominational fellowships where the blood of Christ was preached and the power of Christ was taught. Several opportunities arose in our marriage where the enemy tried to harm our children, and we responded in faith. We understood our faith in Christ put a spiritual target on our backs, so to speak.

While overseas, we went through tough and turbulent times in our marriage. The Bible says a husband is to love his wife as Christ loved the church. I was disobedient and loved my mistress—my job—more than my wife. The job was my idol and replaced my God. The job was my lover and replaced my wife. The job was my legacy and replaced my children. I sacrificed my Lord, my queen, and my posterity for an employment portfolio. My obsession for professional success consumed my thinking and dominated my heart. My heartlessness was driving my household into the ground.

After leaving federal government service in 2008 and supporting

Jonnel in launching a consulting business in China, my continued immaturity pushed our marriage to a new breaking point. In 2010, Jonnel said it was time to seek godly counseling. Reluctantly, I agreed. I had to come face to face with my sin and tell folks about it. I was humbled. After I was convicted to follow Christ again, Jonnel and I intentionally stopped watching TV and invested that time into studying the Bible in earnest. Within a year, we were leading an international Bible study group and teaching people how to walk by faith and in the power of God—and lives were positively impacted. Through the Word and the Spirit, I was equipped to inspire people, while Jonnel was equipped to challenge people.

REALIZE YOUR OUTCOMES

After you find your God-given calling and proceed to fulfill it through the equipping of the Holy Spirit and Holy Word, you will experience great outcomes. I lead my household and inspire my wife and children to believe in a better tomorrow. We study the Bible together and listen to praise and worship music in our home. The sweetness of God is before our eyes and in our ears on a regular basis.

Great outcomes will spring from fulfilling the two most important commandments cited by Jesus: love God with all your heart, mind, and soul, and love your neighbor as yourself. God told me years ago to write books. I ignored Him and allowed one excuse after another to stop me. To love God is to obey God. I could not say I loved Him while disobeying His command to write books that would propel me deeper into what I was called to *do*, inspire. If I could not fulfill His calling on my life, then there was no point in me retaining the breath of life placed within my lungs.

Finishing this book brought a disobedient chapter of my life to an end, and through the process I learned how to truly love my closest neighbors, my wife, and my children. God softened my hardened heart as I spent more time in His presence, where there is fullness of joy. Observing the two greatest commandments realized a wonderful outcome in my life, family harmony. Success within the home translates into success outside of the home. I am now better positioned to realize more success in the future.

LIVING TO DIE

> But you must ask yourself if you are truly alive if you are not doing what God called you to *do*.

Are you living to die? I know that is a pointed and invasive question. But you must ask yourself if you are truly alive if you are not doing what God called you to *do*. Death must be in your mouth if you find yourself speaking more negative words than positive. Death must be on your mind if you hear yourself thinking more negative thoughts than positive. Death must be in your future if you surround yourself with people who speak and think more negative things than positive. If one of these statements bothers you, you are probably operating in the death cycle and need to switch to the life cycle. Death comes when you are failing—or have failed—to fulfill your God-given calling.

Consider Adam and Eve. God told them they would die by eating fruit from the tree of the knowledge of good and evil. That was a leadership test. Obedience to God is the test of leadership, and they failed. Eating the fruit resulted in them handing over their God-given power to dominate the earth to Satan. Without the power, they could not fulfill their calling to rule and reign over everything God created. The inability to fulfill their calling meant they had to die. Their spiritual death accompanied them throughout their natural life until it squeezed the breath out of their bodies. They spent their waking days living to die.

All people are born dead as a result of Adam and Eve's transgression in the garden of Eden, and thus all people need to be revived. What does this mean? Everyone is born a sinner and *spiritually dead*. Everyone needs to be born again and *spiritually revived*. Accepting Jesus Christ as Lord and Savior revives your spirit and gives you abundant life. However, that is Step 1 in taking back your life and living victoriously. Step 2 is discovering your calling, and Step 3 is fulfilling it. If you do not grow after giving your life to Christ, you will begin to die again. Finding your calling will fuel your will to live. Do not let the sun set on your depression and disappointment. Arrest negative feelings and get back in the game of life. Fulfilling your calling allows you to truly live in God's power and authority.

Each breath we take either promotes spiritual life or spiritual death. It does not matter how many leadership books you read or how many empowerment seminars you attend—nothing fulfills a person like pleasing God. Faith pleases God, and people doing His will demonstrate faith in Him. People doing profitable things with their God-given talent demonstrate faith in Him. Faith enables you to live out God's will for your life and be profitable with your God-given resources. Doing His will and being profitable with His resources is the definition of living. Faith allows you to live, and the righteous are commanded to live by faith (Habakkuk 2:4).

CPR: CALLING, PEOPLE, RESOURCES

> You will not become what God called you to *be* unless you do what God called you to *do.*

If you are one of the many Christians on planet earth today living to die, you need to change your thinking by renewing your mind with the Word of God. The Word says you are to live by faith. Living by faith means you are walking the walk God called you to walk. What path are you supposed to take, and where are you going? Your path is what you are called to *do*, and your destination is what you are called to *be*. You will not become what God called you to *be* unless you do what God called you to *do*. This is why you need to focus on finding and fulfilling your calling.

God may have you become several different things in life. He may have you go to multiple different locations during your walk on earth. However, there is one principal thing He has called you to *do* throughout your entire life, and that is your specific calling. Once you have found your calling, surround yourself with supportive people and gather spiritual resources (e.g., spiritual knowledge, wisdom, and understanding) to help you fulfill it. I call it the Calling, People, Resources principle, or CPR. Embrace it and revive a dead life. Look at your life as a triangle with three points. Each point represents a CPR principle.

See Illustration A.

Calling

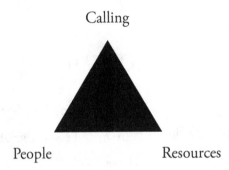

People   Resources

Illustration A

Your God-given calling is at the top of the triangle because it drives the bus. People and resources undergird your calling and help you fulfill it. Supportive people are vital, and their influence on your life cannot be underestimated. You typically reflect the people you have spent the most time around over the past five years. Godly people support a godly lifestyle and promote the life cycle. Ungodly people support an ungodly lifestyle and support the death cycle. The Holy Word and Holy Spirit of God will reveal people who should be in your orbit.

You cannot carry out what God has planned in your own strength; that would be surefire failure. Spiritual resources—spiritual knowledge, wisdom, and understanding—are indispensable. Knowledge is the acquisition and recognition of spiritual insight. Wisdom is the right application of knowledge. Understanding is connecting the dots and seeing the big picture.

And the Holy Word and Holy Spirit of God bring all three spiritual resources—spiritual knowledge, wisdom, and understanding—together.

MY MISTAKE

> As mentioned earlier in this chapter, my mistake was focusing more on what I was called to *be* during a particular season of my life and not on what I knew I was called to *do* throughout my life.

As mentioned earlier in this chapter, my mistake was focusing more on what I was called to *be* during a particular season of my life and not on what I knew I was called to *do* throughout my life. My problem was obsessing over my job, which resulted in neglecting the weightier things in my life, namely my wife and children. Let me be clear. There is nothing wrong with pursuing professional success. It becomes a problem though when the quest for the prize takes you off course and out of the will of God. Your course is your calling, and God desires you to fulfill it. I was called to inspire people to believe in a better tomorrow, but I failed to inspire my own wife and children because I was so focused on my job.

Although I was physically engaged and financially supportive, I was emotionally detached and "not present" at home. Money means nothing in a marriage when hubby is out of touch. I was breaking my vow to love Jonnel as Christ loved the church and digging myself into a deeper hole. My selfishness became a poor witness for Jesus Christ before my closest neighbors, the people in my own home.

Jesus said loving God was the first great commandment and loving your neighbor as yourself was the second. How you treat the people you can see reflects how you treat the God you cannot see. I was pursuing professional success at the expense of my family. My marriage almost disintegrated, and my household nearly collapsed. Not only did I buy the lie presented by Satan, but I owned the wickedness and refused to evict a bad spirit.

I became like one of those people in Matthew 7:22–23 who said "Lord, Lord, have we not prophesied in Your name . . . and done many wonders in Your name?" The truth was that my heart was far from Him and I was out of His will. "I never knew you; depart from Me, you who practice lawlessness!" were the Lord's words that could have been awaiting me at judgment day. I could have been counted among the wretched that thought they could neglect their neighbors and still be right with God. I was wrong, very wrong, and playing with fire. Saved but sinking would have been an apt description of my life during those low points. I had to confess my outright and blatant sin and repent.

Deception covered me like a blanket and I snuggled up with it. I was willfully blind to my sinful attitude and behavior because I was too proud and arrogant to admit wrongdoing. In my mind, I was riding strong on the favor

> I was willfully blind to my sinful attitude and behavior because I was too proud and arrogant to admit wrongdoing.

of God and too high on my horse to come down and see the field of manure I was in. I chose to be deceived with my stinking thinking. My hardened heart did not love God, did not love myself, and did not love my family. It loved pursuing professional success and undermined what He called me to *do*. I was running down the path of sin, which rewards its finishers with death. Deception is ruinous and destructive. Understand what it is and how to overcome it by faith in God.

CHAPTER 2

DECEPTION DESTROYS POTENTIAL

FAITH IS YOUR SHIELD

WHAT DECEPTION IS AND HOW TO OVERCOME IT

To deceive is to lie, and the only way to overcome deception is by faith in the power and authority of Jesus Christ. Satan (also known as the devil), your enemy, deceives by lying. He says untrue things. He twists the truth. He leads people astray. Satan lies to advance his goal, which is your destruction. If he can wreck you, he can wreck the outcomes you were called and equipped to produce. He is committed to distracting and defeating you with false words. Your delusion and death are his desire. Satan is not your friend and does not have your best interests at heart. He is wicked and wrong. The devil hates you and wants you to fail.

> To deceive is to lie, and the only way to overcome deception is by faith in the power and authority of Jesus Christ.

Satan is a liar and a murderer and typically works through people.

You must be on guard and watchful as the enemy seeks to undermine your God-given calling. Do not be deceived by people who are children of the devil and desire nothing more than your downfall. Anyone who denies Jesus Christ as Lord and Savior and does not believe He was raised from the dead for the sins of the world does not love God and has not given their life to God. These people are not children of God but children of Satan. They follow the directions and dictates of the devil. Christ was quite clear with the Pharisees (the Jews who were experts in the law of God given to Moses) who falsely claimed to be children of God. The apostle (special messenger) John's Gospel reveals the truth Jesus communicated: the Pharisees were children of Satan:

> You are doing the works of your [own] father. They said to Him, We are not illegitimate children and born out of fornication; we have one Father, even God. Jesus said to them, If God were your Father, you would love Me and respect Me and welcome Me gladly, for I proceeded (came forth) from God [out of His very presence]. I did not even come on My own authority or of My own accord (as self-appointed); but He sent Me. Why do you misunderstand what I say? It is because you are unable to hear what I am saying. [You cannot bear to listen to My message; your ears are shut to My teaching.] You are of your father, the devil, and it is your will to practice the lusts and gratify the desires [which are characteristic] of your father. He was a murderer from the beginning and does not stand in

the truth, because there is no truth in him. When he speaks a falsehood, he speaks what is natural to him, for he is a liar [himself] and the father of lies and of all that is false. (John 8:41–44 AMPC)

Deception is the tool Satan uses to steal, kill, and destroy your calling, equipping, and outcomes potential in Christ Jesus. Dreams are dashed and hope is lost when the devil succeeds. You must be strong in the Lord to resist demonic attacks against your spirit, soul, and body. The enemy fears God, and you—as a child of God—represent the power of the Almighty, which is greater than the power of the enemy. The enemy will fear you too if you know who you are in Christ Jesus and how to release the power of God. Jesus Christ, the Son of God, is all-powerful and crushed the enemy through His crucifixion and resurrection.

> Deception is the tool Satan uses to steal, kill, and destroy your calling, equipping, and outcomes potential in Christ Jesus.

It is our covenant right as children of Father God to inherit the victory of Christ over Satan and walk in the power of God. God did not create His people to be punching bags and hockey pucks for the enjoyment and amusement of the evil one. Jesus destroyed the works of the enemy and enabled mankind to be reconnected with God. It is our responsibility to learn about the power and authority we have in Christ Jesus to prosper and produce results pleasing unto God.

The blood Jesus shed during the crucifixion and the word of the testimony that God resurrected Him from the dead overcame Satan. When we believe in our hearts that Jesus paid for our sins with His blood and testify with our mouths that God raised Christ from the grave, we are saved. Salvation makes power available. To be saved means to be delivered from the kingdom of darkness into the kingdom of light. God desires all men to be saved, which is why He sent Jesus to die for everyone. And that means everyone. No one is exempted from the love of God and denied an opportunity to receive Jesus Christ as Lord and Savior.

Everyone has a choice to follow Jesus or Satan. Everyone has a choice to enter heaven or hell. Life and death are before each of us and God wants us to choose life. Life is for the obedient and righteous, for they love God and have given their lives to Him. Death is for the rebellious and

> Everyone has a choice to follow Jesus or Satan.

wicked, for they do not love God and have not given their lives to Him. Be humble and turn your heart toward the Lord. Do not be prideful and harden your heart toward the Lord. He loves you and knows the hurt, pain, and emptiness you feel. He desires for you to walk in dominion and be more than a conqueror. You have the ability—through Christ—to diffuse the devil's deception.

Here are three steps to accessing and releasing God's power and authority to overcome deception:

Step #1: The first step is to understand the position of God. Father God, Jesus Christ (the Word of God), and the Holy Spirit jointly constitute God. Father God is the head and is greater than Jesus Christ and the Holy Spirit. God is the Creator of the universe and enthroned in heaven. The earth is His footstool and He is all-powerful. He is the great I AM and has no beginning or end. He created all of us and knows the days of our lives. Nothing is unknown to God. We have no secrets from Him and cannot hide from Him. He knows the thoughts and intents of our hearts. There is absolutely no expectation of privacy before Him as he knows everything about us. You might be able to fool yourself, but you cannot fool God.

Step #2: The next step is to understand the position of Satan. The devil is the wicked one who roams the earth seeking whom he may deceive. He was given the legal right and authority to run wild and create problems until he is cast into the Lake of Fire and tormented forever. There is nothing Satan can do to reverse the judgment of eternal condemnation against him. He seeks to eliminate you—and any seed you may have—from the earth because his time is short and he wants to take as many spirits with him to the place of no return.

Step #3: The final step is to understand your position. If you have made Jesus Christ your Lord and Savior, then you are part of the body of Christ and are joined to the Lord. You have been crucified and resurrected with Jesus Christ and sit together with Him at the right hand of Father God. You are positioned with Christ in heaven and have access to the same power and authority He has because you are connected to God through the sacrifice of His blood. Jesus hung on the cross for us and accepted punishment for our sins. As a result, you have the power of God available to you and authority over the devil and demonic spirits seeking to deceive you. Jesus declared His people have power and authority over the enemy in Luke 10:17–20:

> The seventy returned with joy, saying, Lord, even the demons are subject to us in Your name! And He said

to them, I saw Satan falling like a lightning [flash] from heaven. Behold! I have given you authority and power to trample upon serpents and scorpions, and [physical and mental strength and ability] over all the power that the enemy [possesses]; and nothing shall in any way harm you. Nevertheless, do not rejoice at this, that the spirits are subject to you, but rejoice that your names are enrolled in heaven. (AMPC)

What are you afraid of? You do not need to fear engaging Satan and hosts of demonic spirits if you love God with all of your heart and have given your life to Him. Jesus defeated the enemy and gave us the right to walk in that victory. Christ stepped down from heaven to give up His life and give us abundant life here on earth:

I am the Door; anyone who enters in through Me will be saved (will live). He will come in and he will go out [freely], and will find pasture. The thief comes only in order to steal and kill and destroy. I came that they may have and enjoy life, and have it in abundance (to the full, till it overflows). I am the Good Shepherd. The Good Shepherd risks and lays down his [own] life for the sheep. (John 10:9–11 AMPC)

> God loves you and wants all of you, not part of you.

God loves you and wants all of you, not part of you. This means He wants your body, mind, and soul. He wants your time, family, and career. He wants to be the first and foremost part of your life. He wants you exclusively to Himself. His love is more than enough to heal your broken heart and oppressed mind. Remember, the greatest deception Satan can pull on you is to convince you to believe God does not love you and has not given you enough. This is exactly the snare he set for Eve in the garden of Eden. His trickery and lies persuaded her to believe God did not love her and was withholding something of value from her. Eve was easy prey for a cunning and crafty predator. Do you want victory? Do you want prosperity? Do you want peace? Understand what deception is, and respond in faith when Satan brings it.

FAITH IS YOUR SHIELD

Faith is your defense against Satan. He *cannot* overcome a person in faith. Although his words are his weapons, his arsenal is no match for the person who trusts in God. God is greater than Satan, and His power is released through faith. The challenge for the believer today is to stand firm, immovable. You must be rooted and grounded to prevail. Faith is your shield and enables you to withstand Satan's attacks. Understand you are in a battle and must fight. The enemy hurls arrows at you in hopes of inflicting harm and landing a fatal strike. Earthly knowledge and weapons have no effect. Only spiritual knowledge and weapons are effective. Paul the Apostle said we wrestle with demonic spirits—not people—and urged Christians to put on and use the whole armor of God in his letter to the church at Ephesus.

> Faith is your defense against Satan.

Finally, my brethren, be strong in the Lord and in the power of His might. Put on the whole armor of God, that you may be able to stand against the wiles of the devil. For we do not wrestle against flesh and blood, but against principalities, against powers, against the rulers of the darkness of this age, against spiritual hosts of wickedness in the heavenly places. Therefore take up the whole armor of God, that you may be able to withstand in the evil day, and having done all, to stand. Stand therefore, having girded your waist with truth, having put on the breastplate of righteousness, and having shod your feet with the preparation of the gospel of peace; above all, taking the shield of faith with which you will be able to quench all the fiery darts of the wicked one. And take the helmet of salvation, and the sword of the Spirit, which is the word of God; praying always with all prayer and supplication in the Spirit, being watchful to this end with all perseverance and supplication for all the saints. (Ephesians 6:10–18 NKJV)

Satan is a spirit-being, and you are a spirit-being. The battle is in the spirit realm and not in the natural world. You wrestle against spirits and not people. I know this might sound strange, but it is the truth. What we cannot see is more real than what we can see. Satan led praise and worship in heaven when he was the angel Lucifer and took many angels with him when he fell from grace. He is the master of seduction and knows how to deceive. The prophet Isaiah writes about the fall of Lucifer:

> How you are fallen from heaven, O Lucifer, son of the morning! How you are cut down to the ground, You who weakened the nations! For you have said in your heart: "I will ascend into heaven, I will exalt my throne above the stars of God; I will also sit on the mount of the congregation On the farthest sides of the north; I will ascend above the heights of the clouds, I will be like the Most High." (Isaiah 14:12–14 NKJV)

The apostle John sheds light on what happened in heaven in the revelation of Jesus Christ:

> And war broke out in heaven: Michael and his angels fought with the dragon; and the dragon and his angels fought, but they did not prevail, nor was a place found for them in heaven any longer. So the great dragon was cast out, that serpent of old, called the Devil and Satan, who deceives the whole world; he was cast to the earth, and his angels were cast out with him. (Revelation 12:7–9 NKJV)

Like a lion on the hunt, Satan's instinct is to attack and destroy. People—especially the children of God—are his targets. The devil is ruthless and vicious and shows no mercy. He plans and executes battle plans to bring about your downfall and defeat. Please know he can succeed if you have no knowledge of the fact that you already have victory in Christ Jesus! Satan can always take down a person who is willfully ignorant of the power available to them through Christ. Lack of knowledge destroys the people of God (Hosea 4:6).

Warfare is a zero-sum game for Satan; his gain is your loss, and your gain is his loss. Do not underestimate his ability to deceive through words—he will use persuasive rationale for the path he wants you to take. Thousands of years of human responses to his strategies and tactics are in his database. Countless kingdoms and billions of people have come and gone during his reign on earth. He has some key knowledge but is devoid of wisdom and understanding. This is where you have an advantage as God can provide invaluable insight on navigating the battlefields and engaging the enemy. Seek His face daily for fresh perspective and discernment on how to stand strong in faith amid madness.

FAITH REPELS SATAN

Faith in God causes Satan to flee. When you stand in faith, you stand in the power of God. When you resist in faith, you resist in the power of God. When you speak in faith, you speak in the power of God. The enemy of your soul is simply no match for the Father of your spirit.

Submission to God is the path to victory. Humility and obedience yield wisdom and understanding, which opens your eyes to spiritual truths. Despite

> Faith in God causes Satan to flee.

natural facts, truth prevails. The devil cannot deceive a person who loves God and has given their life to Him. The following Scriptures from the apostle Peter and brother James (the bondservant of God and Jesus Christ), respectively, reveal how the devil operates and how the people of God should respond:

> Be sober, be vigilant; because your adversary the devil walks about like a roaring lion, seeking whom he may devour. Resist him, steadfast in the faith, knowing that the same sufferings are experienced by your brotherhood in the world. (1 Peter 5:8–9 NKJV)

> So be subject to God. Resist the devil [stand firm against him], and he will flee from you. Come close to God and He will come close to you. [Recognize that you are] sinners, get your soiled hands clean; [realize that you have been disloyal] wavering individuals with divided interests, and purify your hearts [of your spiritual adultery]. (James 4:7–8 AMPC)

How do you draw close to God? Think, speak, and do what pleases God. How do you know what pleases God? Live by faith. How do you live by faith? Be led by the Holy Spirit. How can you be led by the Holy Spirit? Build up the spirit of faith within you. How can you build up the spirit of faith within you? Hear the Word of God. How can you hear the Word of God? Listen to it being preached, for "faith comes by hearing, and hearing by the word of God" (Romans 10:17 NKJV).

Know the Word of God, believe the Word of God, and speak the

Word of God. This is how you deal with—and overcome—temptation. Temptation comes to everyone, and you are no exception. The question is whether you will succeed or fail amid the moment. Satan is the tempter and will come with deceptive words designed to snare you. What do you do when this happens? Do what Jesus did and respond in faith by knowing, believing, and speaking the Word of God. Satan tried—but failed—to tempt Jesus. The gospel account according to Matthew describes how the Lord handled an encounter with Satan:

> Again, the devil took Him up on an exceedingly high mountain, and showed Him all the kingdoms of the world and their glory. And he said to Him, "All these things I will give You if you will fall down and worship me." Then Jesus said to him, "Away with you, Satan! For it is written, 'You shall worship the LORD your God, and Him only you shall serve.'" Then the devil left Him, and behold, angels came and ministered to Him. (Matthew 4:8–11 NKJV)

You cannot fake faith. Satan knows whether you possess the power or not. God has made His strength available to anyone who will receive it. All you must do is reach out and accept it. It is a free gift ready to be appropriated and activated. Why not act right now? It does not make sense to walk in weakness when you can walk in strength. Have faith in God and walk. Do not think you can resist the temptation of the enemy with your mind or muscle.

You cannot fake faith.

Resistance is futile without faith, and faith works through love: "For in Christ Jesus neither circumcision nor uncircumcision avails anything, but faith working through love" (Galatians 5:6 NKJV).

HOW EVE WAS DECEIVED

Eve was deceived. But how was that possible since she was created directly by God? Eve was not born a sinner, like you and me. She was created without sin and had no knowledge of evil (as far as we know). However, she was given the power to choose and chose to follow Satan and not God. How did that happen? Eve lacked love toward God. All disobedience flows from not loving God. When you love God, you obey Him and abide in Him. Jesus shared this truth with the disciples after the Last Supper:

> All disobedience flows from not loving God.

> "If you love Me, keep My commandments. And I will pray the Father, and He will give you another Helper, that He may abide with you forever—the Spirit of truth, whom the world cannot receive, because it neither sees Him nor knows Him; but you know Him, for He dwells with you and will be in you. I will not leave you orphans; I will come to you. A little while longer and the world will see Me no more, but you will see Me. Because I live, you will live also. At that day you will know that I am in My Father, and you in Me, and

I in you. He who has My commandments and keeps them, it is he who loves Me. And he who loves Me will be loved by My Father, and I will love him and manifest Myself to him." Judas (not Iscariot) said to Him, "Lord, how is it that You will manifest Yourself to us, and not to the world?" Jesus answered and said to him, "If anyone loves Me, he will keep My word; and My Father will love him, and We will come to him and make Our home with him. He who does not love Me does not keep My words; and the word which you hear is not Mine but the Father's who sent Me. These things I have spoken to you while being present with you. But the Helper, the Holy Spirit, whom the Father will send in My name, He will teach you all things, and bring to your remembrance all things that I said to you. (John 14:15–26 NKJV)

You might ask how is it possible to obey God in this modern-day and digital age when worldly wisdom and seductive influences can be accessed through handheld devices in seconds. You might wonder how someone can abide in God when cultural norms of speech and dress throughout the world are too often laced with rebellious and sensual connotations. There is an answer to these lines of inquiry: be led by the Holy Spirit of God. Freedom from the bondage and fear of the world is available to those who trust God and follow His Spirit. The apostle Paul revealed this powerful point in his letter to all the saints in Rome:

For as many as are led by the Spirit of God, these are sons of God. For you did not receive the spirit of bondage again to fear, but you received the Spirit of adoption by whom we cry out, "Abba Father." The Spirit Himself bears witness with our spirit that we are children of God, and if children, then heirs—heirs of God and joint heirs with Christ, if indeed we suffer with Him, that we may also be glorified together. (Romans 8:14–17 NKJV)

Father God sent the Holy Spirit to be with His children and lead them in the way of righteousness. The Holy Spirit will clarify for you the difference between the wisdom of God and the wisdom of man. The Holy Spirit will tell you how to think, speak, and act in a manner that pleases God. The Holy Spirit will teach you how to deal with family members, work colleagues, team members, and others who may be challenging and difficult. A teacher is a speaker. The Holy Spirit will speak to you. Position yourself to hear clearly. Build up your spirit—which is a measure of the Holy Spirit residing within you—through praise and worship, prayer, and Bible study. Speak to God, and He will hear you. The Holy Spirit of God will speak to your spirit. The question is whether you will listen and obey.

Are you unsure about what to do with your life? Are you unclear about what to do with your career? Are you unresolved about what to do with your significant other? The Holy Spirit has the answers and will give you the peace about what to do. This peace might not make any natural sense, but it will resonate with your heart and mind if you humble yourself before God. Have the mind of Christ, which was humble and obedient, and you will be able to accept the hard truth about your situation. Walk in the truth, and be set free from the bondage of fear.

Now, let us delve into Adam and Eve. God (Father, Son, and Holy Spirit) created them in His likeness and image and gave them the power to rule and reign over the earth. This was an intentional move by the Creator of the universe to have living beings similar to Him. Mankind was neither an accident of nature nor a product of evolution. Men and women were placed on earth for a purpose. They were called to succeed, reproduce, and conquer. Moses recorded the entrance of Adam and Eve on the planet earth in the first book of the Bible he wrote, Genesis:

> Then God said, "Let Us make man in Our image, according to Our likeness; let them have dominion over the fish of the sea, over the birds of the air, and over the cattle, over all the earth and over every creeping thing that creeps on the earth." So God created man in His own image; in the image of God He created him; male and female He created them. Then God blessed them, and God said to them, "Be fruitful and multiply; fill the earth and subdue it; have dominion over the fish of the sea, over the birds of the air, and over every living thing that moves on the earth." (Genesis 1:26–28 NKJV)

Adam and Eve were capable of loving God. However, being made in His likeness and image did not compel them to love Him. The capacity to love did not result in the conviction to love. Eve had a choice, and she chose not to love God. How do we know this? She did not keep the commandment of God, which was to not eat from the tree of the knowledge of good and evil. She did not love Adam either, as she offered him the same forbidden fruit.

Eve knew the Word of God, but did not believe it. Although she spoke it, no power flowed out and she did not do what she was told to do. Eve made the mistake of lending her ear to the voice of the enemy who challenged whether the commandment she heard was true. His deceptive words, mixed with her heart of unbelief, resulted in his elevation and her subjugation. Satan destroyed her potential to administer the earth with Adam through deception.

> Eve knew the Word of God, but did not believe it.

Do you love God or do you love the world? The answer is seen in actions of obedience or disobedience. Loving God results in keeping His commandments, but loving the world results in *not* keeping His commandments (a commandment is anything God says to do or not to do). When we keep His commandments, we show we love and know Him. However, if we say we know God but do not keep His commandments, we walk in deception and untruth. The apostle John outlined these principles in a beautiful letter he wrote about what he—and others—heard and saw with their own eyes about the Word of life, Jesus:

> Do you love God or do you love the world?

Now by this we know that we know Him, if we keep

His commandments. He who says, "I know Him," and does not keep His commandments, is a liar, and the truth is not in him. But whoever keeps His word, truly the love of God is perfected in him. By this we know that we are in Him. (1 John 2:3–5 NKJV)

Do not love the world or the things in the world. If anyone loves the world, the love of the Father is not in him. For all that is in the world—the lust of the flesh, the lust of the eyes, and the pride of life—is not of the Father but is of the world. (1 John 2:15–16 NKJV)

By this we know that we love the children of God, when we love God and keep His commandments. For this is the love of God, that we keep His commandments. And His commandments are not burdensome. (1 John 5:2–3 NKJV)

Deception is the ultimate fruit of not loving God. Let us go deeper into the story of what happened in the garden of Eden and reveal the truth. As noted previously, God made mankind (Adam and Eve) in His likeness and image. The first family had God's attributes and character upon creation and a level of godly knowledge, divine wisdom, and spiritual understanding. God does not make anything imperfect. They were pure and natural from the start. But did they remain like that?

> Deception is the ultimate fruit of not loving God.

God did not make a robot called Adam and a robot called Eve. He created a man named Adam and a woman named Eve. They were not preprogrammed sacks of dirt but people capable of making their own decisions. God told Adam (and by extension Eve since she was still within Adam) to not eat from the tree of the knowledge of good and evil, and that eating from it would result in death. This was the only tree in the entire garden of Eden that was off limits. The tree of life was also in the garden, and they were free to eat from it. God's direction regarding the troublesome tree can be seen in Genesis 2:16–17:

> And the Lord God commanded the man, saying, You may freely eat of every tree of the garden; But of the tree of the knowledge of good and evil and blessing and calamity you shall not eat, for in the day that you eat of it you shall surely die. (AMPC)

Satan (in the body of a serpent) told Eve the exact opposite of what God said. He said she would *not* die from eating from the tree of the knowledge of good and evil, which was a lie. Eve disobeyed God and obeyed Satan. She accepted the temptation, ate the fruit, and was duped. She gave some to Adam, and he ate it as well. Adam and Eve's eyes were opened, and they fell from grace due to pride, the same reason Satan fell. As noted earlier in this chapter, Satan was previously an angel in heaven named Lucifer. He was created by God and led other angels in divine praise and worship. He thought he was better than God and was kicked out of heaven. He was cast down to earth and permitted to run around until the day of his eternal punishment. Eve became a slave to Satan and was condemned to die. God warned her about the consequence of disobedience, but she ignored the wisdom from above and ate the forbidden fruit. But why would she do that?

PRIDE, UNFORGIVENESS, FEAR, AND LOVELESSNESS

Eve was prideful. But how was that possible since she was the first of her kind (a female) created by the master of perfection, God? She chose to believe Satan over God. Eve esteemed the words of the serpent over the words of the Creator. She decided to be led by a smooth-talking serpent that offered her something she did not possess: worldly wisdom. She said the fruit from the tree looked good, was good to eat, and desirable to make one wise. To be clear, Eve disregarded the spiritual wisdom of God and sought the sensual wisdom of the world. The wisdom of God appeals to your spirit. The wisdom of the world appeals to your senses. She possessed godly wisdom but lacked worldly wisdom. Light and darkness cannot dwell together. Eve believed wielding worldly wisdom was better than walking with God. When darkness is embraced, light goes out and life slips away. Pride exalts the world and its way of thinking over God and His way of thinking. But what produced her pride?

Eve harbored unforgiveness. She was not happy that God said do not eat from the tree of the knowledge of good and evil. Eve believed He was holding something back and denying the desire of her heart. She thought God wronged and rejected her because He told her not to do something she wanted to do. God was being too strict, too hard, and too difficult in her eyes. Eve wanted to get out from under His rule, and the fruit from that tree was her ticket to self-rule. Eve allowed her selfish desire to be

Eve was prideful.

Eve harbored unforgiveness.

free from God to turn her against Him. She walked in unforgiveness toward God because she believed He was wrong and she was right. With this state of mind, she was easy prey for the predator who captured her soul through words and not war. But why would she think God was trying to keep her down?

Eve was fearful. She suffered from a bad case of FOMO (Fear of Missing Out). Instead of believing that God was looking out for her best interests, she was afraid of not experiencing what worldly wisdom had to offer. Fear is the absence of trust in God. It is a twisted understanding of your identity and a false interpretation of your situation. Negative thoughts, words, and deeds are associated with fear. But why did she possess fear?

Eve lacked love. Love is a choice, and she chose not to love God. Love is a lifestyle, and she chose to walk in the wisdom of the world and not in the wisdom of God. If she loved God, she would have obeyed Him. True love requires humility and

Eve lacked love.

obedience. People who love God choose to honor His Word over their desire. They decrease for Him to increase in their lives. Such people bow before God and follow His commandments.

Unfortunately, Eve was not this person. She was blessed with the strength to choose a Spirit-led life but traded it for the weakness that accompanies self-rule. Eve elevated herself and her desire over her God and His will. She was incapable of giving herself over to her Maker because she chose herself over Him. Things would have been different had she heeded the following reality: the "created" will never be greater than the "Creator" (see Isaiah 29:16; Romans 1:25). Had she accepted this truth and walked in it, she could have avoided deception.

Love prevents fear. Walk in love and avoid the consequences of choosing fear. Fear yields unforgiveness, unforgiveness produces pride, and pride results in deception, which brings pain and suffering. Deception takes root in a heart with pride.

Love prevents fear.

Temptation comes and leads people astray when they see themselves as more important than God. This is pride, and it happens when obeying the Word of God is exchanged for obeying the word of man.

Whether that man is you or another person, accepting the words of the "created" over the words of the "Creator" will result in bondage and slavery. When you disobey and turn away from God, you invite temptation to chain you up and haul you away to the slave master called deception. The truth about deception, though, is that you cannot be deceived without your consent. That statement is shocking and should stop you in your tracks. Think about it: you are conspiring with Satan when you allow yourself to be deceived. The prophet Jeremiah wrote about this relationship between consent and deception. Prophets who were supposed to communicate God's truth, known as prophecy (a declaration about what will happen in the future), instead spoke lies:

The truth about deception, though, is that you cannot be deceived without your consent.

> Then the Lord said to me, The [false] prophets proph-
> esy lies in My name. I sent them not, neither have I
> commanded them, nor have I spoken to them. They

prophesy to you a false or pretended vision, a worthless divination [conjuring or practicing magic, trying to call forth the responses supposed to be given by idols], and the deceit of their own minds. Therefore thus says the Lord concerning the [false] prophets who prophesy in My name—although I did not send them—and who say, Sword and famine shall not be in this land: By sword and famine shall those prophets be consumed. And the people to whom they prophesy shall be cast out in the streets of Jerusalem, victims of famine and sword; and they shall have none to bury them—them, their wives, their sons, and their daughters. For I will pour out their wickedness upon them [and not on their false teachers only, for the people could not have been deceived except by their own consent]. (Jeremiah 14:14–16 AMPC)

Contrary to what many may think, deception is a two-way street, involving both a speaker (leader) and a hearer (follower). There must be a "deceiver" who speaks lies intended to seduce people into thinking the wrong way. By necessity, there must also be a "deceived" person who hears and accepts the lies. Acceptance can come in the form of mental agreement, verbal agreement, or action-oriented agreement, which simply means doing something in agreement with the deception (such as eating forbidden fruit).

> Contrary to what many may think, deception is a two-way street, involving both a speaker (leader) and a hearer (follower).

To be deceived is to be led astray. The heart of the hearer is the key—it can accept or reject what is heard. A loveless and faithless heart will follow wicked and ungodly leadership. God was Eve's leader, not Satan. Eve decided to leave God and follow Satan when she ate the fruit because her heart desired to be free from God. Perhaps she did not know being free from God meant being a slave to Satan. Every human being is born with a desire to worship and be led. God wants us to worship Him and be led by Him. He does not want us to worship Satan and be led by him. Unfortunately, too many people replace God with the false wisdom of the world. The irony is that the wisdom of the world is foolishness to God.

Lack of love toward God, fear of missing what the world offers, unforgiveness toward God or man, pride, and deception are paths to pain, suffering, and eventually death. It is not worth it. Choose life. Father God loved you and gave Himself to you through the Lord Jesus Christ. Reciprocate by loving God and giving yourself to Him. Joy, peace, and happiness will overflow, overwhelm, and overtake you.

EVE'S SEED

It may seem as if I am throwing the book at Eve and being unduly harsh. Condemning her for her pride, unforgiveness, fear, lovelessness, and consent to deception sounds hard. In the bigger picture, Eve was clearly a special person who was singled out by the devil. It cannot be underscored enough how important her role was in

> The enemy sought to deceive Eve, and not Adam, in a vain attempt to derail the divine plan of God.

the eventual coming of the Lord Jesus Christ the Messiah, who was her precious Seed. The enemy sought to deceive Eve, and not Adam, in a vain attempt to derail the divine plan of God.

The book of Revelation gives insight into what Satan knew about the offspring of the woman:

> Now a great sign appeared in heaven: a woman clothed with the sun, with the moon under her feet, and on her head a garland of twelve stars. Then being with child, she cried out in labor and in pain to give birth. And another sign appeared in heaven: behold, a great, fiery red dragon having seven heads and ten horns, and seven diadems on his heads. His tail drew a third of the stars of heaven and threw them to the earth. And the dragon stood before the woman who was ready to give birth, to devour her Child as soon as it was born. She bore a male Child who was to rule all nations with a rod of iron. And her Child was caught up to God and His throne. (Revelation 12:1–5 NKJV)

Satan understood a male child was to come from the woman and rule over all the nations. Because he possessed this knowledge after being cast down to the earth, he was and is laser-focused on attacking the woman and her offspring. Revelation 12:13–17 provides the following narrative:

Now when the dragon saw that he had been cast to the earth, he persecuted the woman who gave birth to the male Child. But the woman was given two wings of a great eagle, that she might fly into the wilderness to her place, where she is nourished for a time and times and half a time, from the presence of the serpent. So the serpent spewed water out of his mouth like a flood after the woman, that he might cause her to be carried away by the flood. But the earth helped the woman, and the earth opened its mouth and swallowed up the flood which the dragon had spewed out of his mouth. And the dragon was enraged with the woman, and he went to make war with the rest of her offspring, who keep the commandments of God and have the testimony of Jesus Christ. (NKJV)

The enemy knew exactly what he was doing when he approached Eve with his deceptive words. He knew she would die from eating the forbidden fruit. The devil thought her death would stop the male child from coming to strip him of his reign over the earth, which began when Adam and Eve obeyed him and not God. This is why God cursed the serpent and declared the victorious coming of Jesus Christ, saying he would "put enmity Between you and the woman, And between your seed and her Seed; He shall bruise your head, And you shall bruise His heel" (Genesis 3:15 NKJV).

CHAPTER 3

FAITH REALIZES POTENTIAL

HAVE FAITH IN GOD

Jesus, the holy Seed of Eve destined to crush the devil's head, urged His disciples to have faith in God. While taking a walk with them one morning, He taught on the importance of having faith in God:

> So Jesus answered and said to them, "Have faith in God. For assuredly, I say to you, whoever says to this mountain, 'Be removed and be cast into the sea,' and does not doubt in his heart, but believes that those things he says will be done, he will have whatever he says. Therefore I say to you, whatever things you ask when you pray, believe that you receive them, and you will have them. And whenever you stand praying, if you have anything against anyone, forgive him, that your Father in heaven may also forgive you your trespasses. But if you do not forgive, neither will your Father in heaven forgive your trespasses." (Mark 11:22–26 NKJV)

Faith in God realizes your calling, equipping, and outcomes potential in Christ Jesus. You must have it to succeed on the path He placed before you. Without faith, you cannot please God and fulfill your purpose. We understand this truth from the following New Testament verse: "But without faith it is impossible to please Him, for he who comes to God must believe that He is, and that He is a rewarder of those who diligently seek Him" (Hebrews 11:6 NKJV).

God formed your flesh and bones and launched your life. He separated you from the womb of your mother to run a race only you could run. He called you out of darkness to play a role only you could play. He granted you grace to do a job only you could do. Do you realize how valuable and special you—yes you—are in the eyes of God? He sacrificed Jesus for you, sculpted unique lines on the tips of your fingers, and numbered every hair on your head.

There is no one like you on the entire earth. Regardless of whether you have a twin sibling and look like someone else in the flesh, you have a different spirit and will be held

> There is no one like you on the entire earth.

accountable for your own actions. You are not responsible for what anyone else does or does not do. Your thoughts, words, and deeds belong to you and you alone. You can stand alone and not be held back by any person, place, or thing. You have free will and can choose your path. Such an awesome opportunity to be "the first you" and not "the next someone else" also carries a level of responsibility with it that should make you feel both special and sober.

The principal common denominator between you and every person on earth is the Holy Spirit. God breathed into man the breath of life, His Holy Spirit, and man became a living being. The core differentiating factor between you and everyone else in the world is your God-given calling. The Lord has a wonderful plan intended for your life for you to own and execute. If you want to stand out from over seven (7) billion people on the planet earth today, then learn about God's plan for your life. Whether you are simple or complex, there is a unique role designed for you to perform on earth.

Here is a question for you. What is your calling? Finding it is like discovering pure gold, which is beautiful and attractive. Like Jesus, God placed you on earth to do a job and return to heaven when it is complete. You have a right to know why you are here. It is not a mystery to be solved upon your deathbed. Your calling is your purpose, which is seen with the eyes of understanding and a heart of faith. Open your eyes and heart and receive from the Lord.

But perhaps you already know your purpose and have grasped it. If that is you, then there is another question. What are you doing to fulfill your calling? A pot of gold will not change your situation unless you do something with it. God has given everyone a talent to use to create value in the world. However, you must invest what was given to you in a productive and useful manner. Gold in the ground is worthless unless it is dug up and used.

Now, you may be someone who has done what God has said and are at the point where your calling is almost, or already, fulfilled. If you are in that category, then there is yet another question. What are you doing to help others find and fulfill their calling? A lifetime of achievement and victory is a great curriculum to use and teach those who are willing to listen. If you know your calling and are on the path to fulfillment, you have important knowledge, wisdom, and understanding to share with others. Doing so will bless those around you and promote life within you.

Many years ago, I visited Israel with a group of committed Christians, and a trip to the Dead Sea (Salt Sea) was a tour stop. We were in the middle of the desert in a desolate place, but the sky was blue and the sun was shining. It was a beautiful day in the Holy Land. A retired Israeli military general was our tour guide, a tough, no-non-sense kind of guy. He was firm, direct, and knowledgeable. While describing the area, he said the Jordan River flowed into the Dead Sea. That was a nice geographical fact, but not earth-shattering.

However, the next thing he said hit me like a bombshell. In fact, it became one of the most explosive pieces of revelation I ever received. He said the Dead Sea had no outlet. Wow! This sea was dead because it always received and never released. This is just like the human body. No matter how healthy certified organic food is for your body, you cannot keep consuming it without passing it. You will be as dead as the Dead Sea if you do not release what you receive. This is not only true for your natural health but also for your spiritual health. Your growth in the spirit realm will be stunted if you do not pass on what you have learned. Speak life into another person and sow righteous seeds in their heart. It will profit them and yield a har-

> You will be as dead as the Dead Sea if you do not release what you receive.

vest for you.

Finding and fulfilling your calling is a faith journey. There is great potential bound up inside of you. But what are you doing to realize it? Faith in God is the key to unlocking your greatness. Activate your faith with the Word of God (Jesus Christ) and the Spirit of God (Holy Spirit). They are the partners you need to make your calling real. Ministers are charged with equipping saints for the work of ministry and reaching the lost. Simply put, preachers and teachers are supposed to train the people of God to grow in their knowledge of the Word and Spirit of God. The purpose is to bless all people and impact the world for Christ. God equipped you to fulfill the greatness placed in your heart. You are His handiwork and more important than any sun, moon, or planet created in the cosmos. However, you and you alone are responsible for realizing your full potential.

Your calling, equipping, and outcomes potential in Christ Jesus will be realized on earth when you walk through the three-phase process of discovering your calling, developing your calling, and delivering results. Your faith in God will bring each dimension into harmonious alignment. When you discover your calling and develop it through spiritual equipping, you will deliver outstanding results. Successful professional athletes often demonstrate how this process works as the discovery and development of their natural talent produces impressive statistics.

> Your calling, equipping, and outcomes potential in Christ Jesus will be realized on earth when you walk through the three-phase process of discovering your calling, developing your calling, and delivering results.

FAITH IS TRUSTING GOD

When you trust in God, you will take Him at His word. There will be no doubt, fear, confusion, or shame. You will operate in a faithful, consistent, steadfast, and firm manner. There will be no negative thinking, slanderous speaking, or wrong doing. You will have clear thoughts, confident speech, and definite actions. You will look, sound, and feel different. Trusting in God and leaning on His understanding—not yours—is necessary to discover and develop your God-given calling and deliver God-pleasing outcomes. Your full potential can only be realized by trusting in your Creator. God does not want us to trust in man and rely upon our own way of thinking. This would lead us down the wrong path and to a bad result, which is what happened to Eve. The wise sayings of King Solomon tell us where to place our trust:

> Trusting in God and leaning on His understanding—not yours—is necessary to discover and develop your God-given calling and deliver God-pleasing outcomes.

> Trust in the LORD with all your heart, and lean not on your own understanding; In all your ways acknowledge Him, and He shall direct your paths. Do not be wise in your own eyes; Fear the Lord and depart from evil. It will be health to your flesh, and strength to your bones. (Proverbs 3:5–8 NKJV)

People who fully trust in the Lord communicate with Him on a regular basis and receive guidance. Their steps are ordered and their path is illuminated. Joy is their companion and they walk in love. They live in peace and sleep in safety. They have a good name and keep their word. They conduct life in decency and in order. They lead with integrity and experience prosperity. Patience and endurance are their running mates. Success and victory are their cheering squad. Glory and honor are their reward. The eyes of the Lord continually scan the earth searching for people who have the right heart. He seeks those who have faith in Him. Are you positioned to please God right now? It is impossible to do so without faith. Ask yourself this tough question, and find out where you are today: Do you trust God? Your honest answer to that question will reflect the real amount of faith in your heart. Jesus, who knew all men, identified at least four levels of faith: 1) no faith; 2) little faith; 3) faith; and 4) great faith.

Level #1 – No faith

You do not want to be in this category. No faith means no trust in God. These people are not on the same page with God. They are filled with fear and have no hope. Faithless people—and often their children—experience pain, suffering, and sorrow. Look no further than the demon-possessed boy brought to Jesus by his faithless father to understand this truth.

> Now it happened on the next day, when they had come down from the mountain, that a great multitude met Him. Suddenly a man from the multitude cried

out, saying, "Teacher, I implore You, look on my son, for he is my only child. And behold, a spirit seizes him, and he suddenly cries out; it convulses him so that he foams at the mouth; and it departs from him with great difficulty, bruising him. So I implored Your disciples to cast it out, but they could not." Then Jesus answered and said, "O faithless and perverse generation, how long shall I be with you and bear with you? Bring your son here." And as he was still coming, the demon threw him down and convulsed him. Then Jesus rebuked the unclean spirit, healed the child, and gave him back to his father. (Luke 9:37–42 NKJV)

Level #2 – Little faith

You do not want to remain in this zone. Fear has a strong grip on people with little faith. Although "something is better than nothing," you may find yourself pleading for your life and hoping to survive a storm if you have little faith. Consider what happened once when Jesus and the disciples were in a boat on the sea:

Now when He got into a boat, His disciples followed Him. And suddenly a great tempest arose on the sea, so that the boat was covered with the waves. But He was asleep. Then His disciples came to Him and awoke Him, saying, "Lord, save us! We are perishing!" But He said to them, "Why are you fearful, O you of little faith?" Then He arose and rebuked the winds and the sea, and there was a great calm. So the men marveled, saying, "Who can this be, that even the winds and the sea obey Him?" (Matthew 8:23–27 NKJV)

Level #3 – Faith

You can thrive and see miracles in this arena. Physical healing occurs, and faith-filled prayers are answered. Suffering can end and joy can begin, like in the story of the courageous woman determined to connect with Christ:

Now a certain woman had a flow of blood for twelve years, and had suffered many things from many physicians. She had spent all that she had and was no better, but rather grew worse. When she heard about Jesus, she came behind Him in the crowd and touched His garment. For she said, "If only I may touch His clothes, I shall be made well." Immediately the fountain of her blood was dried up, and she felt in her body that she was healed of the affliction. And Jesus, immediately knowing in Himself that power had gone out of Him, turned around in the crowd and said, "Who touched My clothes?" But His disciples said to Him, "You see the multitude thronging You, and You say, 'Who touched Me?'" And He looked around to see her who had done this thing. But the woman, fearing and trembling, knowing what had happened to her, came and fell down before Him and told Him the whole truth. And He said to her, "Daughter, your faith has made you well. Go in peace, and be healed of your affliction." (Mark 5:25–34 NKJV)

Level #4 – Great faith

This is where you want to be . . . and remain! This is where life is snatched from the jaws of death and the power of God is on full display. You have no choice but to prosper and realize your full potential in Christ at this level. The military official's servant who was healed brings this truth to life:

> Now when He concluded all His sayings in the hearing of the people, He entered Capernaum. And a certain centurion's servant, who was dear to him, was sick and ready to die. So when he heard about Jesus, he sent elders of the Jews to Him, pleading with Him to come and heal his servant. And when they came to Jesus, they begged Him earnestly, saying that the one for whom He should do this was deserving, "for he loves our nation, and has built us a synagogue." Then Jesus went with them. And when He was already not far from the house, the centurion sent friends to Him, saying to Him, "Lord, do not trouble Yourself, for I am not worthy that You should enter under my roof. Therefore I did not even think myself worthy to come to You. But say the word, and my servant will be

healed. For I also am a man placed under authority, having soldiers under me. And I say to one, 'Go,' and he goes; and to another, 'Come,' and he comes; and to my servant, 'Do this,' and he does it." When Jesus heard these things, He marveled at him, and turned around and said to the crowd that followed Him, "I say to you, I have not found such great faith, not even in Israel!" And those who were sent, returning to the house, found the servant well who had been sick. (Luke 7:1–10 NKJV)

THE SPIRIT OF FAITH

Faith is a spirit and that spirit is the Holy Spirit. There are only two spiritual dimensions, and they are the kingdoms of light and darkness. A spirit either belongs to one kingdom or the other. The spirit of faith can only be associated with the kingdom of light and never affiliated with the kingdom of darkness. God is a spiritual being and created spiritual beings—men and women—to fellowship with Him. Adam was made in the likeness and image of God and became a living being when God breathed His Holy Spirit into him. God expected Adam to live by faith because Adam had a measure of faith on the inside, which was the Holy Spirit.

> Faith is a spirit and that spirit is the Holy Spirit.

What you do with the measure of faith—the Holy Spirit—entrusted to you will impact what happens to you on earth. It will also determine whether you spend eternity in heaven or hell. Let us look at Scripture with the spirit of wisdom and revelation in the knowledge of Christ and understand the spirit of faith. It has everything to do with your success or failure during this lifetime and your joy or misery in the next.

The Bible says faith is a spirit. In his second letter to the church of God at Corinth, Paul the Apostle made the following statement: "And since we have the same spirit of faith, according to what is written, 'I believed and therefore I spoke,' we also believe and therefore speak, knowing that He who raised up the Lord Jesus will also raise us up with Jesus, and will present us with you" (2 Corinthians 4:13–14 NKJV).

The Bible infers the Holy Spirit is faith. In 1 Corinthians 13:13, it is written that faith, hope, and love abide and that the greatest of these is love. We know Father God, the Word (Jesus Christ), and the Holy Spirit are three-in-one from 1 John 5:7. We know God is love from 1 John 4:8. We know Jesus Christ is our hope from 1 Timothy 1:1 and Titus 2:13. We know Father God is greater than Jesus from John 14:28. Since God is love, and Jesus is hope, it can be discerned that the Holy Spirit is faith. The faith, hope, and love referenced in 1 Corinthians 13:13 refers to the three entities—Father God, Jesus Christ, and Holy Spirit—constituting one God.

Under the inspiration of the Holy Spirit, the unknown author of the New Testament book Hebrews said the following about faith:

> Now faith is the substance of things hoped for, the evidence of things not seen. For by it the elders obtained a good testimony. By faith we understand that the

worlds were framed by the word of God, so that the things which are seen were not made of things which are visible. (Hebrews 11:1–3 NKJV)

Another translation says:

Now faith is the assurance (the confirmation, the title deed) of the things [we] hope for, being the proof of things [we] do not see and the conviction of their reality [faith perceiving as real fact what is not revealed to the senses]. For by [faith–trust and holy fervor born of faith] the men of old had divine testimony borne to them and obtained a good report. By faith we understand that the worlds [during the successive ages] were framed (fashioned, put in order, and equipped for their intended purpose) by the word of God, so that what we see was not made out of things which are visible. (Hebrews 11:1–3 (AMPC)

Faith is a *substance*, not a *sense*. Faith is a *thing*, not a *thought*. Faith is a *confirmation*, not a *consideration*. What *substance* and *thing* serves as a *confirmation* in the spirit realm? The answer is the Holy Spirit of God. He is awesome and everywhere. Although the Holy Spirit is not a *sense*, we can certainly sense His presence. Even though the Holy Spirit

> Faith is a *substance*, not a *sense*. Faith is a *thing*, not a *thought*. Faith is a *confirmation*, not a *consideration*. What *substance* and *thing* serves as a *confirmation* in the spirit realm? The answer is the Holy Spirit of God.

is not a *thought*, we can indeed ponder His power. Even though the Holy Spirit is not a *consideration*, we can definitely contemplate His works. The Holy Spirit was present at the restoration of the earth, at the temptation of Eve, and at the crucifixion of Christ. He was also present at the time of your birth and will be there at the time of your death. The great news is He is present with you today and prepared to lead you into tomorrow.

LIVE BY FAITH

What are you going to do with the measure of the Holy Spirit within you? Are you going to place your spirit of faith in the wisdom of men or in the power of God? It is your choice and God wants you to make a good decision. In Paul's letter to the church at Corinth, he addressed this pertinent question saying his speech and [his] preaching were not with persuasive words of human wisdom but in demonstration of the Spirit and of power, that [the Corinthians'] faith should not be in the wisdom of men but in the power of God (1 Corinthians 2:4–5 NKJV).

God wants you to trust Him and not man. God wants you to choose life and not death. God wants you to serve Him and not the enemy. But what do you want to do? Do you want to succeed in life? Do you want to walk in health? Do you want to prosper financially? Most people would answer "yes" to these questions. If you are one of these people, choose today to live by faith. Living by faith yields stunning success, glowing health, and overflowing prosperity. It also makes people happy, free, confident, patient, and kind. Living by faith is a great lifestyle. However, it is a choice with responsibility attached. You must operate within the will of God and refrain from walking according to the ways of the world. You cannot love God and the world. You must decide where you stand. Sitting on the fence is not an option.

Live by faith and you will discover and develop your calling and deliver outcomes pleasing unto God. It is just that simple. The will of God is not a mystery to those whose hearts are pure before Him. Trust in God, and every single step you need to take will be clear and illuminated, no guesswork. Confusion is not of God as it results from a spirit of pride. Fear is not of God as it springs from a lack of love. What is the state of your heart? Is it riddled with pain, sorrow, and anxiety? Is it feeling depressed, oppressed, or possessed? Is it cursing the day you were born and wishing you were dead? If you answered "yes" to any of the previous questions, stop what you are doing right now and arrest the negative emotions surrounding your heart. Turn away from the storm coming your way and say, "Jesus is Lord" again, and again, and again. Speak *this* truth until it becomes *your* truth. Doing so will halt the deception, disperse the darkness, and defeat the devil.

> Live by faith and you will discover and develop your calling and deliver outcomes pleasing unto God.

About six hundred years before the birth of Jesus Christ, God spoke the following words through the prophet Habakkuk to the people of God:

And the Lord answered me and said, Write the vision and engrave it so plainly upon tablets that everyone who passes may [be able to] read [it easily and quickly] as he hastens by. For the vision is yet for an appointed time and it hastens to the end [fulfillment]; it will not deceive or disappoint. Though it tarry, wait [earnestly] for it, because it will surely come; it will not be behindhand on its appointed day. Look at the proud; his soul is not straight or right within him, but the [rigidly] just and the [uncompromisingly] righteous man shall live by his faith and in his faithfulness. (Habakkuk 2:2–4 AMPC)

God did not present a new *living by faith* doctrine through the prophet Habakkuk. Adam and Eve were called to live by faith, which was living by the Holy Spirit, from the first day they walked the earth. The Holy Spirit was on the scene when the earth was restored and was present in the garden of Eden with the first family. God breathed the breath of life—the Holy Spirit—into their empty earth vessels, and they became living beings. They walked and talked because the Holy Spirit dwelt within and provided life. God blessed Adam and Eve when He told them to be fruitful, multiply, fill the earth, and subdue it. They could only fulfill this calling through the Holy Spirit. They could not even follow biblical Scripture because Genesis—the first book of the Bible—was not written until Moses came over one thousand years later!

Adam and Eve had the spirit of faith residing within them and the freedom to choose whether to put their faith in the wisdom of man or in the power of God. God wanted them to be led by His Holy Spirit, but they opted to follow the lustful desire of their flesh—the desire to possess earthly wisdom—instead. Life and death were before them in the form of the tree of life and the tree of the knowledge of good and evil, respectively. Despite being commanded to choose life, they chose death and ate from the tainted tree. They did not love God enough to be humble and obedient. Adam and Eve did not please God because they lived by the flesh and not by faith.

God calls every Christian to live by faith. This *universal* calling has been the central gospel message since the earth was restored. Its importance has been

> God calls every Christian to live by faith.

underscored at least three times in the New Testament—in Romans, Galatians, and Hebrews—as Habakkuk's *living by faith* Scripture:

> For in the Gospel a righteousness which God ascribes is revealed, both springing from faith and leading to faith [disclosed through the way of faith that arouses to more faith]. As it is written, The man who through faith is just and upright shall live and shall live by faith. (Romans 1:17 AMPC)

> Now it is evident that no person is justified (declared righteous and brought into right standing with God) through the Law, for the Scripture says, The man in right standing with God [the just, the righteous] shall

live by and out of faith and he who through and by faith is declared righteous and in right standing with God shall live. (Galatians 3:11 AMPC)

But the just shall live by faith [My righteous servant shall live by his conviction respecting man's relationship to God and divine things, and holy fervor born of faith and conjoined with it]; and if he draws back and shrinks in fear, My soul has no delight or pleasure in him. (Hebrews 10:38 AMPC)

Every Christian is called to walk in love. Love enables the *universal* calling of *living by faith* to be fulfilled. Since faith is required to please God and faith works by love, love is the path to pleasing God. This should not be a surprise as God is love and you are to imitate Him. You are called to love God, love your neighbor, love other Christians, and love your enemies. Fulfill the love commandment, and open the door to understanding your purpose.

> Fulfill the love commandment, and open the door to understanding your purpose.

Jesus taught about the importance of loving God and loving your neighbor in a conversation with a scribe:

Then one of the scribes came, and having heard them reasoning together, perceiving that He had answered them well, asked Him, "Which is the first commandment of all?" Jesus answered him, "The

first of all the commandments is: 'Hear, O Israel, the
LORD our God, the LORD is one. And you shall love
the LORD your God with all your heart, with all your
soul, with all your mind, and with all your strength.'
This is the first commandment. And the second, like
it, is this: 'You shall love your neighbor as yourself.'
There is no other commandment greater than these."
(Mark 12:28–31 NKJV)

Every Christian has been equipped with the Word of God and the
Holy Spirit of God. Doing the Word and following the Spirit with a
pure heart will cause you to walk in love. As previously noted, love
makes faith work, and faith pleases God. In addition to the *universal*
calling of *living by faith*, every Christian has a *specific* calling. You are
called to do something unique before
you die. Find out what this is from
God. Study the Word of God daily with
a humble heart, and receive knowledge,
wisdom, and understanding on how to

> In addition to the
> *universal* calling of *living
> by faith*, every Christian
> has a *specific* calling.

find and fulfill your specific calling. Worship God daily with an obedient heart and receive instruction from the Holy Spirit on how to carry
out your calling step by step. Speak the Word of God over your life, do
what the Holy Spirit says, and you will prosper in all your ways.
Outcomes you cannot imagine will occur in your life.

FAITH IN ACTION: ABEL

The Holy Spirit (spirit of faith) realized the potential people had in God. It moved many people to do amazing things or have awesome experiences. Regardless of whether faith or the Holy Spirit was explicitly mentioned in a passage, scriptural context and discernment reveal the truth. Faith has been at work in the lives of people since God restored the earth. Consider Abel and the role of the Holy Spirit in his life from the contexts of Genesis and Hebrews:

> And Adam knew Eve as his wife, and she became pregnant and bore Cain; and she said, I have gotten and gained a man with the help of the Lord. And [next] she gave birth to his brother Abel. Now Abel was a keeper of sheep, but Cain was a tiller of the ground. And in the course of time Cain brought to the Lord an offering of the fruit of the ground. And Abel brought of the firstborn of his flock and of the fat portions. And the Lord had respect and regard for Abel and for his offering, But for Cain and his offering He had no respect or regard. So Cain was exceedingly angry and indignant, and he looked sad and depressed. (Genesis 4:1–5 AMPC)

> [Prompted, actuated] by faith Abel brought God a better and more acceptable sacrifice than Cain, because of which it was testified of him that he was righteous [that

he was upright and in right standing with God], and God bore witness by accepting and acknowledging his gifts. And though he died, yet [through the incident] he is still speaking. (Hebrews 11:4 AMPC)

Genesis does not mention the role of faith but Hebrews does. Neither mention the Holy Spirit. Does that mean the Holy Spirit was not present? No. We know the Holy Spirit was on the scene because He hovered over the face of the waters when the earth was without form (Genesis 1:2). Hebrews says faith prompted Abel to give God an accept-

> Faith *caused* Abel to do something pleasing unto God.

able sacrifice. Faith *caused* Abel to do something pleasing unto God. Abel was a righteous prophet according to Jesus (Matthew 23:34–35). Prophets speak about the future through the Holy Spirit. Righteous sons of God are led by His Holy Spirit (Romans 8:14). People are sons of God through faith in Christ (Galatians 3:26). The Holy Spirit prompted Abel, a righteous son of God, to give an acceptable sacrifice to God even though Genesis does not reference the Holy Spirit.

FAITH IN ACTION: ENOCH

Evidence of the Holy Spirit (spirit of faith) at work can also be seen in Enoch, who was in the seventh generation from Adam. Like, Abel, Enoch prophesied and pleased God. He walked with the Lord and was led by the Holy Spirit. Not much is written in the Bible about this faithful man. However, Genesis and Hebrews provide insight on his life-changing experience:

> When Enoch was 65 years old, Methuselah was born. Enoch walked [in habitual fellowship] with God after the birth of Methuselah 300 years and had other sons and daughters. So all the days of Enoch were 365 years. And Enoch walked [in habitual fellowship] with God; and he was not, for God took him [home with Him]. (Genesis 5:21–24 AMPC)

> Because of faith Enoch was caught up and transferred to heaven, so that he did not have a glimpse of death; and he was not found, because God had translated him. For even before he was taken to heaven, he received testimony [still on record] that he had pleased and been satisfactory to God. (Hebrews 11:5 AMPC)

As we saw with Abel, Genesis does not mention the role of faith with Enoch—but Hebrews does. Also, neither mentions the Holy Spirit. Hebrews indicates that Enoch did not die and was taken up to heaven *because* of faith. This is an excellent example of the spirit of faith, the Holy Spirit, in action. The Holy Spirit took Enoch from earth and brought him to heaven, alive. That is not hard to believe since the Holy Spirit took Jesus from heaven and brought him to earth alive. Second Kings 2 details another account of a

> Hebrews indicates that Enoch did not die and was taken up to heaven *because* of faith.

faithful man avoiding death and being transferred to heaven. A whirl-wind encompassed the prophet Elijah and delivered him to heaven. The whirlwind was the physical manifestation of the Holy Spirit.

FAITH IN ACTION: NOAH

Amid an entirely corrupt and wicked world, Noah was a righteous man who walked with God. He had the potential to save his family from a catastrophic flood and replenish the earth with the human race. Noah had no idea that worldwide destruction was on the horizon. His trust in God enabled him to hear clearly from God:

> And God looked upon the world and saw how de-generate, debased, and vicious it was, for all humanity had corrupted their way upon the earth and lost their true direction. God said to Noah, I intend to make an end of all flesh, for through men the land is filled with violence; and behold, I will destroy them and the land. Make yourself an ark of gopher or cypress wood; make in it rooms (stalls, pens, coops, nests, cages, and compartments) and cover it inside and out with pitch (bitumen). (Genesis 6:12–14 AMPC)

> [Prompted] by faith Noah, being forewarned by God concerning events of which as yet there was no visible sign, took heed and diligently and reverently con-structed and prepared an ark for the deliverance of his

own family. By this [his faith which relied on God] he passed judgment and sentence on the world's unbelief and became an heir and possessor of righteousness (that relation of being right into which God puts the person who has faith). (Hebrews 11:7 AMPC)

> However, we see from Scripture that the Holy Spirit (spirit of faith) *caused* Noah to take what God said seriously and build the ark.

As it was with Abel and Enoch, Genesis does not mention the role of faith with Noah, but Hebrews does. Again, neither book mentions the Holy Spirit. However, we see from Scripture that the Holy Spirit (spirit of faith) *caused* Noah to take what God said seriously and build the ark. His obedience paid off as his family was saved and the earth was repopulated through his sons.

JESUS IS LORD

The vision every Christian should have today is this: Jesus is Lord. Decide today that everything in your life will revolve around Christ (and not the other way around). Write it down on a piece of paper and tell people about it. Ask God what changes must be made in your life to align everything with Christ. Eliminate wrong thinking, negative words, and bad habits—they undermine your vision. Disconnect (in love) from toxic people, twisted relationships, and tainted partnerships. Step out of darkness and into the light. Think correct thoughts, speak positive words, and do good deeds. Connect (in wisdom) with righteous people, form pure relationships, and negotiate healthy partnerships. These actions taken together will manifest the glory of God in your life, which will show and prove Jesus is your Lord.

When Jesus is your Lord, the specific reason you are on earth shall be—or become—obvious. What you need to think, say, and do will be clear. The people you need to be in league with will appear. The relationships you need to have will manifest. The partnerships you need to work through will materialize. Do not be discouraged, though, if God meets each of these "needs" in different seasons. Do not worry if the specific vision for your life takes a long time to realize. Although you are on your journey, it might not be on your preferred timetable. Why? Life happens. Some people or things might need to be in place before your next move. Some challenges or setbacks might need to be overcome before progress can be made. Whatever the circumstance, God knows exactly where you are and what must happen to move you forward.

Be sure to address the greatest threat to your progress, which is you. Nothing can stop the plan of God for your life like you can. Nothing can stop God from making something happen in your life like you can. Get out of your way and let God have His way. Your life will be better off

> Be sure to address the greatest threat to your progress, which is you.

when you step aside and die to your old ways of thinking, speaking, and doing. The past is dead, but God is not. He is alive and will renew you daily with His Holy Spirit, if you allow Him to do it. Do not be arrogant and proud. God stays far away from those folks. They are destined to fail and have no inheritance in the kingdom of God. There is no light in their heart and no hope in their soul. They are unrighteous to the core and set against God. Sin is their friend and death is their comforter. Be humble and obedient. This is the state of mind Jesus had when he walked on the earth and faced trials, tribulations, and temptations. Jesus loved God and existed to do His will. Jesus was righteous and lived by faith. Be like Jesus!

Be like Jesus!

FAITH RELEASES POWER

LIFE OR DEATH

D o you have faith in God or man? Here is another way to put it: Do you trust in the knowledge of God or in the knowledge of the world? Depending on where you place your faith, you will release either the power of life or the power of death. If you are looking to prosper and eventually hear the Lord say, "well done thy good and faithful servant," then place your faith in what God says. If you are looking to self-destruct and follow Satan, then put your trust in what man says. The Spirit of God opposes the spirit of the world. Jesus was hated by the spirit of the world when He walked the earth because He refused to be seduced and deceived into choosing death. He chose to be humble and obedient before God, and chose life. What is awesome is that He decided to die for all of us, which resulted in everyone having the option to choose life.

LACK OF (GODLY) KNOWLEDGE DESTROYS

My people are destroyed for lack of knowledge. Because you have rejected knowledge, I also will reject you from being priest for Me; Because you have forgotten the law of your God, I also will forget your children. (Hosea 4:6 NKJV)

The people of God die for lack of knowledge, according to the Word of the Lord through the prophet Hosea. This "knowledge" is the knowledge of God, and it's obtained by choosing Him. You choose God when you are humble and obedient before Him. You become humble and obedient before Him when you love Him and give Him your life. God is waiting for you to choose Him. The moment you do so, he opens His storehouse of knowledge, wisdom, and understanding. He stores up these precious and invaluable jewels for those who are just and right in His eyes.

> The people of God die for lack of knowledge, according to the Word of the Lord through the prophet Hosea.

Eve sought the knowledge of the world and was seduced into thinking the tainted fruit would make her wise. Disregarding the instruction of God was not a viable option. She violated the law God laid down because she did not value Him or His commandment. Eve was probably a beautiful woman who was intelligent. However, her disobedience resulted in her rejecting the knowledge of God and God Himself. Therefore, she was punished. She was called to live in the garden of Eden and commune with God. That life was destroyed. You cannot reject God and dwell in His presence. The heavenly Father will not force anyone to be with Him. You must choose your path. Choose wisely.

The allure of worldly knowledge enticed Eve to spurn her Creator and embrace her deceiver. She turned from the lover of her soul and pivoted to the enemy of her spirit. She went from freedom to slavery. As a result, she was rejected by God and ejected from the garden of Eden with her husband Adam. She forgot the law of God and yielded to the word of Satan. No wonder her firstborn, Cain, had anger issues and murderous intent. Cain gave God an offering of the fruit of the ground, but God did not accept Cain or his offering. In contrast, Abel gave God an offering of the first of his livestock and of their fat portions, and God accepted Abel and his offering. Cain was wicked and riotous, while Abel was righteous and prophetic. Cain stewed over being rejected and in revenge killed Abel in the field. Perhaps Eve thought God had forgotten her children, as she had forgotten Him.

> The allure of worldly knowledge enticed Eve to spurn her Creator and embrace her deceiver.

POSSESSION OF (GODLY) KNOWLEDGE BUILDS UP

Therefore I also, after I heard of your faith in the Lord Jesus and your love for all the saints, do not cease to give thanks for you, making mention of you in my prayers: that the God of our Lord Jesus Christ, the

Father of glory, may give to you the spirit of wisdom and revelation in the knowledge of Him, the eyes of your understanding being enlightened; that you may know what is the hope of His calling, what are the riches of the glory of His inheritance in the saints, and what is the exceeding greatness of His power toward us who believe, according to the working of His mighty power which He worked in Christ when He raised Him from the dead and seated Him at His right hand in the heavenly places, far above all principality and power and might and dominion, and every name that is named, not only in this age but also in that which is to come. And He put all things under His feet, and gave Him to be head over all things to the church, which is His body, the fullness of Him who fills all in all. (Ephesians 1:15–23 NKJV)

Faith enables you to obtain the knowledge of God. Pray for the spirit of wisdom and revelation to be upon you and other faithful people in Christ Jesus. It is the will of God for you to understand His will for your life. Why would He create billions of people on earth and not tell them their purpose? God desires full fellowship with all people. Everyone

> Faith enables you to obtain the knowledge of God.

was made in His likeness and image and has an opportunity to know Him through Jesus Christ. When you choose God, you are choosing His way of doing things. This is far better than the way of the world.

The Word of God brings light into your spirit. Master the Word, and you will not be confused. Open your eyes and see the glory and goodness of the Lord in the land in which you live. He longs to dominate your heart and share His plans for your life. Your issues and irritations will fizzle in the presence of His love, grace, and mercy. The power residing within His Word is beyond your natural comprehension. Study the Word daily, and you will renew the spirit of your mind. Remember, the Word is Jesus Christ. The Spirit of Christ, which is the Holy Spirit, will come upon you in a powerful way and lead you down the right road. All you need to do is trust in the Lord. Have faith in God and see His power released in your life.

Jesus Christ is the cornerstone of our existence on earth. We are best served when we build upon the solid rock. Grow in the Word of God, and you will grow in the knowledge of God. Except for the Father, Jesus is above everything in the natural and spiritual realms. His name ranks higher than anything named in the past, present, or future. He is in the power position, and we are right there with Him. He was our substitute upon the cross when He was crucified. God credited His death to us, which means we do not need to die "for" our sins. Jesus saved us from that punishment and gave us grace. However, we must have faith in God and die "to" our sins if we want to dwell in heaven after our bodies expire on earth. Resist the devil by faith, and do not yield your thoughts, words, and deeds to him. Satan wants you to curse people in your mind, offend people with your words, and seduce people with your body. This is all sin and has no place in the life of a Spirit-filled member of the body of Christ.

EVE RELEASED DEATH . . .

Eve had faith in the knowledge of the world and released the power of death and destruction in her life. The tree of life and the tree of the knowledge of good and evil were both amid the garden of Eden. Pay special attention to the names. Please note it was *not* the "tree of the knowledge of life" and the "tree of good and evil" in the famous garden. It was the "tree of life" and the "tree of the knowledge of good and evil." If Eve chose to follow God and ate fruit from the tree of life, she would have received the knowledge of God and lived forever without sin. Instead, she chose to follow Satan, ate from the tree of the knowledge of good and evil, and died that day. Although her physical body was alive, her spirit was dead. Death flowed out of her womb until Christ came and broke the chain. Christ, the chain-breaker, was without sin but became sin to pay the price of sin for the entire world. That was no easy task and His life was required by Father God to satisfy the wages of sin, which is death.

> Eve had faith in the knowledge of the world and released the power of death and destruction in her life.

> Now then, we are ambassadors for Christ, as though God were pleading through us: we implore you on Christ's behalf, be reconciled to God. For He made Him who knew no sin to be sin for us, that we might become the righteousness of God in Him. (2 Corinthians 5:20–21 NKJV)

... BUT ADAM COULD HAVE CONTAINED IT

At first blush, it is easy to lay the fall of mankind squarely at the feet of Eve. After all, she was the one who was deceived and not Adam. She took the first bite of the fruit, not Adam. Death reigned on the earth because of her disobedience, right? Wrong. God held Adam accountable for that, not Eve. Regardless of what Eve did, Adam decided to heed her voice over God and mankind suffered as a result. God creates leaders, supplies them with power (His Holy Spirit), and gives them instructions (His Holy Word). The leader is responsible for fulfilling his/her calling in Christ and accepting the consequences of disobedience.

Adam was fashioned by God, empowered with the breath of life, and tasked to guard the garden of Eden. God would not have given Adam the responsibility to protect territory without the power and authority to do so. Adam was the supreme leader on earth but failed to remove the serpent from the garden. He disobeyed God and ate the tainted fruit. The ground was cursed because of his wrongdoing and he was sentenced to live by the sweat of his brow. Even though Eve released death and destruction, Adam could have contained it by not accepting her food offering. It is possible she could have been cleansed of her sin and restored through her husband's obedience. Unfortunately, that did not happen. Adam was the leader and

> God would not have given Adam the responsibility to protect territory without the power and authority to do so.

held responsible for death reigning on earth. Only Jesus Christ could override Adam's act and restore the power and authority mankind had over the devil. Romans reveals this truth.

> For if because of one man's trespass (lapse, offense) death reigned through that one, much more surely will those who receive [God's] overflowing grace (unmerited favor) and the free gift of righteousness [putting them into right standing with Himself] reign as kings in life through the one Man Jesus Christ (the Messiah, the Anointed One). Well then, as one man's trespass [one man's false step and falling away led] to condemnation for all men, so one Man's act of righteousness [leads] to acquittal and right standing with God and life for all men. For just as by one man's disobedience (failing to hear, heedlessness, and carelessness) the many were constituted sinners, so by one Man's obedience the many will be constituted righteous (made acceptable to God, brought into right standing with Him). (Romans 5:17–19 AMPC)

CHRIST RELEASED LIFE . . .

Jesus Christ destroyed the works of the enemy and released the power of life. His birth, death, and resurrection were all a testimony of the love of God. Despite the failure of Adam to protect his wife (he could have cast the serpent out of the garden), and the inability of Eve to shield her husband (she could have not offered the tainted fruit to Adam), God brought forth Jesus to heal the pain of

> Jesus Christ destroyed the works of the enemy and released the power of life.

sin and restore the loss of fellowship. Jesus was the plan of God all along as the coming of Christ was ordained prior to the fall of mankind in the garden. Through the love of God, mercy and truth came through Jesus Christ.

The same Holy Spirit who hovered over the waters and entered Adam at his creation was the same Holy Spirit who hovered over the Jordan River and came upon Jesus at His baptism. The Holy Spirit enabled Adam and every person born of Adam's flesh to live and breathe upon the earth. The Holy Spirit empowered Jesus and every person born of the Spirit of Christ (Holy Spirit) to minister and heal upon the earth. After Jesus came to a synagogue in Nazareth, He read the following from the book of the prophet Isaiah:

> The Spirit of the LORD is upon Me, Because He has anointed Me to preach the gospel to the poor; He has sent Me to heal the brokenhearted, to proclaim liberty to the captives and recovery of sight to the blind, to set at liberty those who are oppressed; to proclaim the acceptable year of the LORD. (Luke 4:18–19 NKJV)

Jesus ministered to the lost and healed the sick during His time on earth. He was the living and breathing Word of God and spoke life and power into people during His ministry. The Word of God is full of light and devoid of darkness. When God spoke His Word in the beginning, the heavens and the earth were created. When Jesus spoke His Word two thousand years ago, the sick and the lame were healed. When we speak His Word today, the wisdom and power of God is revealed. Do not undervalue the light and life contained in the Word, which is holy, precious, and special. Be good stewards of the breath of life in your lungs. You cannot speak without using the breath God gave you. Use your breath to proclaim the gospel of God and declare the glory of God. Talk about truth—how God loved the world enough to sacrifice His Son—and it will set people free. Be like Jesus and speak life!

. . . BUT SATAN COULD NOT RESTRAIN IT

Satan tried to stop Jesus from coming to the earth. He knew God had a plan he would not like when the Lord God said the seed of the woman would bruise his head. Satan influenced Cain to kill Abel, the man who pleased God with his faith. However, God blessed Eve with Seth, another seed, in lieu of Abel. The devil waged war against the Jews for thousands of years hoping to stop the Lord before He began His ministry on earth, but failed.

The Holy Spirit came upon a faithful Jewish virgin named Mary and impregnated her with Jesus Christ, the Savior of the world. Mary birthed the Lord in Bethlehem during King Herod's reign. Committed to killing Christ, Herod ordered all male children in Bethlehem under the age of two at that time to be executed. Warned by God in a dream, Joseph escaped with Mary and Jesus to Egypt. After John the Baptist baptized Jesus in the Jordan River, the Holy Spirit led Him into the wilderness to be tested. Satan tried three times to tempt Jesus and end His ministry before it took off. Each time, Christ resisted Satan and declared the Word of God. The devil fled, but returned often to try and destroy Jesus.

Jesus was anointed by God to go about healing people from sickness and delivering people from bondage. He healed many different afflictions and cast out many demonic spirits. Multitudes of oppressed people from Galilee, Decapolis, Jerusalem, Judea, and many other locations came to be restored and set free by the Christ. Paralytics, lepers, and epileptics and blind, deaf, mute, and demon-possessed people flocked to the Lord expecting to receive a miracle. His yoke-destroying power flowed into countless men, women, and children. Faith released His power into the lives of those who were suffering and lost.

> Jesus was anointed by God to go about healing people from sickness and delivering people from bondage.

The devil opposed the works of Christ and sought to destroy Him through a close associate. Knowing how he successfully turned Cain against his brother Abel, Satan filled the heart of Judas Iscariot—one of the twelve disciples of Christ—with greed and hatred. Judas, in an act of cowardice, betrayed his master for thirty pieces of silver. Armed soldiers led Jesus away to Caiaphas the high priest, who conducted an interrogation. Afterward, chief priests and elders bound Jesus and brought Him to Pontius Pilate, who tortured Him and delivered Him up to be crucified. Satan might have thought he won when Jesus hung on the cross, gave up His Spirit, and descended to the belly of the earth. However, God demonstrated His unmatched power and raised His Son Jesus Christ from the dead after three days. Many people saw the resurrected Savior of the world and spoke with Him before He returned to heaven. He is scheduled to return to raise all the dead and gather all the living people in Christ. Eternal life awaits those who chose life.

> Then Peter opened his mouth and said: "In truth I perceive that God shows no partiality. But in every nation whoever fears Him and works righteousness is accepted by Him. The word which God sent to the children of Israel, preaching peace through Jesus Christ—He is Lord of all—that word you know, which was proclaimed throughout all Judea, and began from Galilee after the baptism which John preached: how God anointed Jesus of Nazareth with the Holy Spirit and with power, who went about doing good and healing all who were oppressed by the devil, for God was with Him. And we are witnesses of all things which He did both in the land of the Jews and in Jerusalem, whom they killed by hanging on a tree. Him God raised up on the third day, and showed Him openly, not to all people, but to witnesses chosen before by God, even to us who ate and drank with Him after He arose from

the dead. And he commanded us to preach to the people, and to testify that it is He who was ordained by God to be Judge of the living and the dead. To Him all the prophets witness that, through His name, whoever believes in Him will receive remission of sins." (Acts 10:34–43 NKJV)

THE GOSPEL GROWS FAITH

Romans 10:17 tells us that faith comes by hearing the Word of God. Since the gospel is the Word, faith comes—and grows—from hearing the gospel. The gospel is this good news: people are blessed by God and empowered to succeed by receiving the Spirit of God and the Word of God.

> The gospel is this good news: people are blessed by God and empowered to succeed by receiving the Spirit of God and the Word of God.

After God (Father, Son, and Holy Spirit) created Adam and Eve, He preached the gospel to them. God blessed Adam and Eve and told them to be fruitful, multiply, subdue the earth, and dominate every living creature on it. (Note: Serpents were living creatures, which means Adam and Eve had power over the serpent that slithered into the garden of Eden). God breathed His Holy Spirit and power into Adam and Eve at their creation, then spoke His Holy Word and power over them at their coronation. They were crowned king and queen over the earth and empowered to succeed. They were called by God to rule and reign and equipped by God to conquer everything. Nothing on earth was greater than these two leaders. They were made in the likeness and image of the most powerful being in the universe, God.

Adam and Eve disobeyed God's command, and sin entered the world. Wickedness engulfed the earth and God brought floodwaters to eliminate every person and creature with the breath of the spirit of life. Noah, a descendant of Adam through Adam's son Seth, found grace in God's eyes and was instructed to build an ark to save his family and repopulate the planet. God preached the gospel to Noah after he came out of the ark. He blessed Noah and his sons and give them a charge similar to the one He gave Adam:

> Adam and Eve disobeyed God's command, and sin entered the world.

So God blessed Noah and his sons, and said to them: "Be fruitful and multiply, and fill the earth. And the fear of you and the dread of you shall be on every beast of the earth, on every bird of the air, on all that move on the earth, and on all the fish of the sea. They are given into your hand. Every moving thing that lives shall be food for you. I have given you all things, even as the green herbs. But you shall not eat flesh with its life, that is, its blood. Surely for your lifeblood I will demand a reckoning; from the hand of every beast I will require it, and from the hand of man. From the hand of every man's brother I will require the life of man. Whoever sheds man's blood, By man his blood shall be shed; For in the image of God He made man. And as for you, be fruitful and multiply; Bring forth abundantly in the earth and multiply in it." (Genesis 9:1–7 NKJV)

Noah had three sons, Shem, Ham, and Japheth. Abram (later renamed Abraham by God) was a descendant of Shem. Jesus Christ preached the same gospel message to Abram. He said He would bless Abram and that all the nations of the earth would be blessed through Abram. We know this from what Paul the Apostle wrote to the churches of Galatia:

And the Scripture, foreseeing that God would justify the Gentiles by faith, preached the gospel to Abraham beforehand, saying, "In you all the nations shall be blessed." So then those who are of faith are blessed with believing Abraham. (Galatians 3:8–9 NKJV)

Jesus Christ is the Word of God and became flesh and blood to walk the earth and bless humanity with grace and truth. We know this from the gospel of Jesus according to John the Apostle:

And the Word became flesh and dwelt among us, and we beheld His glory, the glory as of the only begotten of the Father, full of grace and truth. John bore witness of Him and cried out, saying, "This was He of whom I said, 'He who comes after me is preferred before me, for He was before me.'" And of His fullness we have all received, and grace for grace. For the law was given through Moses, but grace and truth came through Jesus Christ. (John 1:14–17 NKJV)

The Word of God is the Scripture of God. Since Jesus Christ is the Word of God, and the Word of God is the Scripture of God, then Jesus Christ is the Scripture of God. This should be clear. If not, consider the transitive property of equality in mathematics for assistance. This property is as follows: If A = B and B = C, then A = C. See Illustration B.

A = Jesus Christ   B = The Word of God   C = The Scripture

If A (Jesus Christ) = B (The Word of God),

and B (The Word of God) = C (The Scripture),

Then A (Jesus Christ) = C (The Scripture)

Illustration B

When Galatians 3:8 said the Scripture preached the gospel to Abraham, it meant Jesus Christ preached the gospel to Abraham.

Understanding this is critical because it helps us see the role of Jesus as recorded in the Old Testament. When Galatians 3:8 said the Scripture preached the gospel to Abraham, it meant Jesus Christ preached the gospel to Abraham. The "in you all the nations shall be blessed" reference in Galatians 3:8 is originally found in Genesis 12:3, which is part of a message from the Lord to Abram. Consider the Genesis account:

Now the LORD had said to Abram: "Get out of your country, From your family and from your father's house, to a land that I will show you. I will make you a great nation; I will bless you and make your name great; And you shall be a blessing. I will bless those who bless you, And I will curse him who curses you; And in you all the families of the earth shall be blessed." (Genesis 12:1–3 NKJV)

The "Lord" who spoke to Abram was the Lord Jesus Christ Himself. As previously noted, Galatians reveals this because it says the *Scripture* preached the gospel to Abram and Jesus Christ is the *Scripture*. Jesus Christ speaking to Abram, as recorded in Genesis 12, may come as an astounding truth to some people. Jesus Christ was active in the affairs of mankind prior to His coming to the earth in flesh and blood to dwell and minister.

The statement "in you all the nations shall be blessed" is the actual good news gospel message as the Holy Spirit was promised to Abraham and his Seed, which was none other than Jesus Christ. Abraham received the promise of the Holy Spirit through faith in God. He trusted God, and his faith realized his potential, which was to bless all nations through his Seed, Jesus Christ. Jesus prophesied about Himself when He preached the gospel to Abraham because He was the Seed of Abraham that the promised

> The statement "in you all the nations shall be blessed" is the actual good news gospel message as the Holy Spirit was promised to Abraham and his Seed, which was none other than Jesus Christ.

Holy Spirit would empower to succeed.

Since Jesus has left the earth and all His believers now constitute His body, the Holy Spirit is also promised to all believers. Therefore, all people today that believe in Jesus and have faith in God, like Abraham, are blessed. When you believe in the Word of God and receive the Holy Spirit, you have the unconquerable power of creation and restoration resident within your spirit. Release this power by speaking the Word of God and walking in the Holy Spirit. Miracles will manifest in your life and in the lives of others. It is impossible for Satan to stop a person who operates in their power and authority in Christ Jesus. Realize the potential of your power today, through faith.

> When you believe in the Word of God and receive the Holy Spirit, you have the unconquerable power of creation and restoration resident within your spirit.

Jesus' mother, Mary, realized the divine power of creation and restoration and blessed the entire world. Her husband, Joseph, was a direct descendant of King David and Abraham. The angel Gabriel visited her, said she was blessed, and prophesied the virgin birth of Christ. Mary received the divine Seed in her womb after choosing to accept the angel's words. Mary conceived and birthed Christ through the Holy Spirit before coming together with her husband. God supplies the Holy Spirit and works miracles when people hear the gospel (good news) and receive it.

Faith in God comes from hearing and believing in the gospel of Jesus Christ, which is also called the gospel of God. The gospel says Christ was crucified for us and is our Lord and Savior. There is power in the blood of Christ. The blood cleansed our sins and healed our sicknesses. The blood delivered us from the kingdom of darkness and transferred us into the kingdom of light. The blood destroyed the yoke of bondage on our necks and freed us to worship God in Spirit and in truth.

Jesus Christ (also known as the Lamb of God) was murdered on the cross outside the gates of the city of Jerusalem. When we accept His blood sacrificed for our lives, God opens our eyes to His power and we understand our victory through Christ. Speak to the enemy from your position of power, and declare your allegiance to God. Doing so will overcome the enemy and yield the breakthroughs needed to succeed in life. The book of Revelation declares the two-fold source of our victory:

> Faith in God comes from hearing and believing in the gospel of Jesus Christ, which is also called the gospel of God.

> Then I heard a loud voice saying in heaven, "Now salvation, and strength, and the kingdom of our God, and the power of His Christ have come, for the accuser of our brethren, who accused them before our God day and night, has been cast down. "And they overcame him by the blood of the Lamb and by the word of their testimony, and they did not love their lives to the death. (Revelation 12:10–11 NKJV)

MIX THE GOSPEL WITH FAITH

Although Romans 10:17 says faith comes by hearing the Word of God, Hebrews 4:2 tells us the Israelites failed in the wilderness because the gospel message they heard did not benefit them because they did not have faith. This raises an interesting question. How can someone grow in faith by hearing the gospel, which is the Word of God, when faith is needed for the gospel to even take root in their heart? This may sound like a chicken and egg situation. Does faith come first or the gospel? The answer is found in Romans 12:3, which says God has given everyone a measure of faith. Therefore, faith comes first.

> Although Romans 10:17 says faith comes by hearing the Word of God, Hebrews 4:2 tells us the Israelites failed in the wilderness because the gospel message they heard did not benefit them because they did not have faith.

For I say, through the grace given to me, to everyone who is among you, not to think of himself more highly than he ought to think, but to think soberly, as God has dealt to each one a measure of faith. (Romans 12:3 NKJV)

Your measure of faith is the spirit of faith God breathed into you. The spirit of faith breathed into you was the Holy Spirit. You cannot live without the breath of God, which is the Holy Spirit, within your lungs. Your measure of faith was given to you before you heard the good news gospel message preached. The spirit of faith dwelling within you is precious and perfect. Are you putting your faith, which is the Holy Spirit, in the power of God or in the wisdom of man? The gospel of God preached today was also preached to the children of Israel. Each Israelite was given a measure of faith but decided not to place it in the power of God but in the wisdom of man. As a result, the gospel message they heard did not take root and grow into a tree of faith. Not believing the gospel of God equates to not believing in God. Those who believed in God entered into His rest, which was heaven. Those who did not believe did not enter into His rest and did not go to heaven. The New Testament letter to the Hebrews reveals these truths.

> So we see that they were not able to enter [into His rest], because of their unwillingness to adhere to and trust in and rely on God [unbelief had shut them out]. Therefore, while the promise of entering His rest still holds and is offered [today], let us be afraid [to distrust it], lest any of you should think he has come too late and has come short of [reaching] it. For indeed we have had the glad tidings [Gospel of God] proclaimed to us just as truly as they [the Israelites of old did when the good news of deliverance from bondage came to them]; but the message they heard did not benefit them, because it was not mixed with faith (with the leaning of the entire personality on God in absolute trust and confidence in His power, wisdom, and good-ness) by those who heard it; neither were they united in faith with the ones [Joshua and Caleb] who heard

(did believe). For who have believed (adhered to and trusted in and relied on God) do enter that rest, in accordance with His declaration that those [who did not believe] should not enter when He said, As I swore in My wrath, They shall not enter My rest; and this He said although [His] works had been completed and prepared [and waiting for all who would believe] from the foundation of the world. (Hebrews 3:19–4:3 AMPC)

THE POWER OF WORDS

Your words have power because they are the fruit of the spirit of faith within your physical body. You cannot release a word without marshaling a puff of air from your lungs. If you do not believe it, take a pause from reading this book and try to speak without pushing air out of yourself. Since the air in your lungs is the breath of life God gave you, you are a steward over His property. He has the power and authority to reclaim His property whenever He so chooses. You are powerless to keep it apart from His will. Your breath is perhaps the most valuable asset you control because you simply cannot live without it. It is a piece of God and powers your mortal body.

> Your words have power because they are the fruit of the spirit of faith within your physical body.

It should be no surprise why your words will either turn on the life cycle or the death cycle. By your words you shall either be saved and live with the Lord forever or be condemned and suffer with the enemy forever. Words matter. Do not let anyone tell you otherwise. People who seek to minimize the importance of words are ignorant and do not have basic knowledge of how things work in either the spiritual or natural realms. God used His words to create the universe and every moon, planet, and star in the cosmos. Satan used his words to snatch control of a planet away from its rightful stewards. Jesus used his words to restore broken bodies and heal broken hearts. People have used words to spread love or spew hate. Words are important. The New Testament letter James, written to fellow believers, highlights how mastering the mouth yields perfection (maturity and wholeness):

> For we all stumble in many things. If anyone does not stumble in word, he is a perfect man, able also to bridle the whole body. (James 3:2 NKJV)

MOSES' ERROR

When God appeared to Moses and told Him what to do, Moses neither believed nor trusted in Him. Initial doubt is the big mistake many great leaders make. If not rectified, it becomes a seed of destruction and diminishes, or brings down, the leader, in some way, shape, or form. God told Moses He came down to deliver His people, the children of Israel,

> When God appeared to Moses and told Him what to do, Moses neither believed nor trusted in Him.

out of bondage. He said He was sending Moses to Pharaoh to bring the children of Israel out of Egypt.

> And Moses said to God, Who am I, that I should go to Pharaoh and bring the Israelites out of Egypt? (Exodus 3:11 AMPC)

Moses questioned his ability to deliver the message of God to Pharaoh and his capability to bring the Israelites up and out of their land of captivity. God responded by saying that He would be with Moses and give him a sign to confirm that He sent him. The sign was that he would serve God on the mountain upon which he stood after bringing the Israelites out of Egypt. Moses then asked God His name, so he could answer the Israelites when they asked. God responded by saying His name is I AM. Then God told Moses to tell the children of Israel that He sent him to them. He instructed Moses to gather together the elders of Israel and tell them God appeared to him to tell them He saw their affliction in Egypt, would deliver them from it, and would send them to a land flowing with milk and honey.

> And [the elders] shall believe and obey your voice; and you shall go, you and the elders of Israel, to the king of Egypt and you shall say to him, The Lord, the God of the Hebrews, has met with us; and now let us go, we beseech you, three days' journey into the wilderness, that we may sacrifice to the Lord our God. (Exodus 3:18 AMPC)

This is significant. God encouraged Moses by saying the elders would heed God's instruction—Moses need only speak the words. Moses and the elders would jointly tell Pharaoh the Lord God of the Hebrews told them he needed to release His people so they could go into the wilderness and sacrifice to the Lord. God informed Moses that when Pharaoh refused, He would stretch out His hand and strike Egypt. In response, Pharaoh would let the Israelites go. They would find favor in the sight of the Egyptians and not leave Egypt poor: they would leave with their designated share of the wealth of the land of their captivity.

This should have been the end of the discussion. Moses should have said "yes, Lord" and left for Egypt with the word he received from God in his mind and the confidence he received from God in his heart. He could have triumphantly entered the camp of the suffering Israelites with the wind at his back and the truth at his side. God said the elders would heed his voice. All Moses had to do was open his mouth and speak exactly what God told him to speak. He did not need to analyze, revise, or summarize. He only needed to speak what he had received. That's it. He did not need to perform a sign or a miracle because God *did not* tell him a sign or miracle was needed for them to heed his voice—only what He told Moses to relay. The Holy Spirit, not Moses, would convince and convict the elders to listen and obey.

The error Moses made was inserting his rebellious self-doubt and unbelief into the picture by thinking that the people might not believe him or listen to his voice (Exodus 4:1). The issue was never about whether the people would believe Moses—rather, the people would believe *God* who said beforehand they would!

The Holy Spirit would have been present to take Moses' words and present them as truth in the elders' hearts. They would have believed after hearing the message. But when Moses doubted, he failed to walk in confidence that his voice was enough, which meant he did not think the Word of God was enough. He wanted to show the people power through signs and wonders. Moses' fear of people rejecting his words resulted in him rejecting the *perfect* will of God, which was to just speak. Unfortunately, Moses did not want to relay God's words to the elders and implored God to send another messenger. His rejection of the *perfect* will of God angered God and resulted in only the *acceptable* will of God being done. God gave him a staff and a spokesperson (his brother Aaron) to stand before the people and Pharaoh and perform signs (Exodus 4:2–17).

> The error Moses made was inserting his rebellious self-doubt and unbelief into the picture by thinking that the people might not believe him or listen to his voice (Exodus 4:1).

You may think this is not a problem. Why would it be an issue to perform signs and miracles so people would believe in them? The answer is straightforward. God wants us to release His power by having faith in Him and speaking His Word. Period. This is His *perfect* will. Since your very breath is the Holy Spirit of God within you, when you speak the Word of God with that breath without doubting, the power of God manifests (Mark 11:22–23). God did not doubt when He said, "Let there be" multiple times and created what we see on, above, and beneath the earth. We were made in His likeness and image. Jesus did not doubt when He commanded things to happen. We can do what

Jesus did, and even greater things.

Now, it may sound like good Christian pep talk to say that your voice and words matter. But do they really? Yes, they do. God wants us to live by the fruit of our mouth and not by the work of our hands. Though He will operate through the work of our hands to bless others, He desires to move through the sound of our voice. Your voice is produced by the Holy Spirit within you. That is higher on the scale of importance than your hands.

> Though He will operate through the work of our hands to bless others, He desires to move through the sound of our voice.

If you are still not sure about this point, look at why Moses retired early from the earth. When the children of Israel were thirsty and asked for water, God told Moses to strike a stone with the staff he held in his hand. Moses obeyed and water flowed out from the rock (Exodus 17:1–7). This was a miraculous sign and wonder. Water came from the rock, and the people's thirst was quenched. Later, when the people's throats became parched again, they cried to Moses for relief. This time, however, God told Moses to *speak* to the rock. He only needed to use his voice. God did *not* say *strike* the rock. Moses would have needed to use his staff.

God wanted Moses to walk in great faith. Great faith operates through the voice of man and not the hand of man.

> Then the LORD spoke to Moses, saying, "Take the rod; you and your brother Aaron gather the congregation together. Speak to the rock before their eyes, and it will yield its water; thus you shall bring water for them out of the rock, and give drink to the congregation and

their animals." So Moses took the rod from before the LORD as He commanded him. And Moses and Aaron gathered the assembly together before the rock; and he said to them, "Hear now, you rebels! Must we bring water for you out of this rock?" Then Moses lifted his hand and struck the rock twice with his rod; and water came out abundantly, and the congregation and their animals drank. Then the LORD spoke to Moses and Aaron, "Because you did not believe Me, to hallow Me in the eyes of the children of Israel, therefore you shall not bring this assembly into the land which I have given them." (Numbers 20:7–12 NKJV)

Unfortunately, in a flash of anger, Moses called the people rebels and struck the rock with his staff. Despite this obvious misstep, the power of God was manifested and people were satisfied.

> Moses died before his time, and people entered the promised land without their leader whom God had called to bring them into the land.

Though God's sheep were cared for, the shepherd's life was cut short. Moses died before his time, and people entered the promised land without their leader whom God had called to bring them into the land. Perhaps the people would not have misbehaved and disobeyed God the way they did in the promised land had Moses lived to lead (Deuteronomy 31:14–21).

CHAPTER 5

NINE CALLING TYPES

LIVE YOUR CALLING

DIFFERENT CALLINGS

Your calling is your life force. Your calling is what you release without conscious effort and intentional thinking. Your calling is not something put forward in a beta test and changed based on feedback. It is what God placed you on earth to do. It is with you during your entire life. Your calling type is what you are called to *do* rather than what you are called to *be*.

To recognize your calling, notice what most people say after interacting with you during your best days. See how most people feel after experiencing your

> Your calling type is what you are called to *do* rather than what you are called to *be*.

best work. The way most people respond to the best of you reflects your calling. This is because God brings out your best.

Finding and fulfilling your calling will position you to avoid making costly mistakes. Do not be like me and get your priorities out of order. What you are called to *do* for God is more important than what you are called to *be* for God. Pride hardened my heart, and I did not accept this truth. I was wrapped up with pursuing positions, power, and praise. I should have sought first the kingdom of God and His righteousness and allowed Him to add the right things to me. He knows exactly what I need and precisely when I need it. By not being humble and obedient, I rejected godly knowledge and wisdom. Natural experience became my task-master when spiritual enlightenment was willing to become my teacher. Although I course corrected and left the path of consequence and calamity, I wasted precious time and energy. It would have been more profitable for me, and others, had I walked in the love of God and submitted to His will.

There are at least nine different types of callings based on scriptural insight related to what you are called to *do*. This was placed within you when God breathed life into you. It does not leave you, regardless of what you do, because it is not based on what you do. It is based on who you are, which was determined by God. You did not make your spirit, He did. You did not determine your purpose on earth, He did.

> There are at least nine different types of callings based on scriptural insight related to what you are called to *do*.

You did not decide what womb to be incubated in, He did. You cannot separate yourself from what you were called to *do* and live, just as you cannot separate yourself from your breath of life and live. Why? The reason is simple. What you were called to do *is* you. This is your heart. This is your unique signature. This is your top strength. This is how you bless people. This is how you best relate to people. This is how you live in peace. You cannot fire yourself. You cannot divorce yourself. You cannot ignore yourself. Learn your calling. Learn your soul. Learn yourself.

Below are nine calling types with a brief description of each and a select biblical figure who exemplified each calling. Profiles of the calling types follow.

Table 1: Nine Calling Types			
	Calling Type	What It Does	Biblical Figure
1	Comforter	Brings peace	Noah
2	Deliverer	Brings freedom	Joseph
3	Conqueror	Brings victory	Joshua
4	Watchman	Brings warning	Ezekiel
5	Inspirer	Brings hope	David
6	Challenger	Brings growth	John the Baptist
7	Builder	Brings security	Nehemiah
8	Worshiper	Brings holiness	Bezalel
9	Sower	Brings revelation	Paul the Apostle

COMFORTER

Comforters bring peace by fulfilling God-ordained covenants. A covenant is an agreement. Comforters who consent to—and perform—an agreement that pleases God are in His will. Favor seems to follow

Comforters bring peace by fulfilling God-ordained covenants.

them wherever they go. They are peace-makers. They have a pleasant demeanor and bring calmness after a storm. Stability and steadfastness are hallmarks of their character. Healing and wholeness flow from their spirit. They comfort and are comforted by words. Integrity and soundness reflect their leadership style. They conduct business with wisdom and guide people with understanding. It is common for them to be pioneers, trendsetters, and trailblazers. They have a heart for the oppressed and the underdog.

While walking in love, comforters are secure in their faith toward God and persistent in most—if not all—of their ways. They are obedient, faithful followers and passionate, fearless fighters. Faith-filled mountaintop experiences dot their spiritual landscape. Dogged determination to uphold an agreement and keep their word is the norm. They have an abundance of patience and compassion. Their forgiveness knows no boundaries. Active listening, effective communication, and sincere empathy are their strengths.

When operating in godlessness, comforters can be lustful and seductive. They can be persecutors and not protectors. Unchecked fear can bring them down to the pit of disgrace and cause them to be unkind and untrustworthy. Lack of attention to detail and reliance upon unfaithful people can be their weaknesses. They should be rooted and grounded in God. Conquerors can be great counterparts for a comforter and help them remain focused.

DELIVERER

Deliverers bring people from slavery to freedom. Whether it is spiritual, mental, or physical bondage, deliverers specialize in breaking captive's chains and leading them to the shores of liberty. They see suffering and are moved to act. Standing still in the face of injustice and tyranny is not an

> Deliverers bring people from slavery to freedom.

option. Deliverers are activists by design and seek the greater good. Self-sacrifice is the price they are willing to pay for others to be free. They often embrace a lifetime commitment to a single cause. They are praised for their prowess, hailed for their heroism, and revered for their discernment.

When deliverers walk in the Spirit, heaven and earth seem to move as captives are set free after years, decades, or even centuries of bondage. Dedicated to relieving pain and suffering, they have no problem confronting wickedness and promoting godliness. Grounded in a sense of justice, they pursue their purpose until the work is finished. They are strong, reliable, fair, and forthright. Lives are transformed and hope is restored when they flow in the power of God.

In the absence of godliness, deliverers can be dictatorial, dismissive, or deceptive. Idolatry can flourish in their presence and people led by deliverers can lose control if the deliverers persist in sin. Bitterness and rebelliousness can take root in their heart if plans go awry. They should prioritize understanding the spirit realm and being led by the Holy Spirit. Worshippers can serve as effective counterbalances for deliverers by helping them stay humble.

CONQUEROR

Conquerors wage war and win battles. God uses these warriors to overcome enemy forces with raw power and might. Most—if not all—of their campaigns are victorious. Sound strategy and tactics are vital to their success. Courageous and consistent, they execute plans well and stay focused on achieving established objectives. Conquerors often embrace a militaristic zero-sum game mentality. They tend to see the world in black and white, rather than in shades of gray, and admire strength and sacrifice. Weakness and compromise are undesired in their book. Conquerors easily accept a challenge and take charge and are bold.

> Conquerors wage war and win battles.

However, it can be difficult for such a person to admit wrong, take ownership, and apologize. Passion and vision drive them to engage and overcome challenges.

In the Spirit, conquerors are impressive, effective, and magnificent. They possess winning attitudes, hold firm beliefs, and envision conclusive victories. They demonstrate strength, resilience, and relentlessness in their endeavors. Confidence, conviction, and clarity are heard in their speech. Diligence, decisiveness, and determination are seen in their actions. Power, authority, and might are felt in their presence.

If they do not walk in love, conquerors can be destructive, demeaning, and draining. They can be impatient, reckless, and foolish. Poor discernment and bad decisions can undermine their objectives. Arrogance and ill-advised alliances can be their downfall. Lack of self-control can result in destabilizing behavior. They should seek after godly wisdom as it will help them make the best decisions. They are drawn to other conquerors to fight a common enemy and need comforters to help heal after a fight.

WATCHMAN

Watchmen warn of impending danger and urge people to act. Bowing down and praying for righteousness amid iniquity is their responsibility. Standing guard and sounding the alarm when the enemy appears is their role. Walking with God and discerning His will in difficult situations is their mandate. Writing and/or speaking the Word of God in a timely and truthful manner is essential to their influence and effectiveness. While serving as monitors, advisors, or overseers, these people urge others to live, work, and play in an ethical and honorable manner. They stress how actions and attitudes today shape outcomes and results tomorrow. They prescribe strategies and tactics to change a course of action and avoid failure.

> Watchmen warn of impending danger and urge people to act.

When yielded to the Holy Spirit, watchmen have 20/20 vision, see future threats, and communicate actionable solutions. They say the right words to the right people at the right time. They have a reputation for being reliable and resilient under pressure. They possess deep convictions and pure intentions. Attentiveness and responsiveness mark their character.

If ungodly, watchmen can be corrupt, insensitive, and ignorant. Laziness and complacency can fester within their heart if they lose sight of their purpose. They can fall into the trap of talking the talk but not walking the walk. They must guard against honoring man above God. As the enemy will seek to corrupt their offspring, they must correct their children when they are wrong. It is important for them to maintain a sense of urgency, but not anxiety. Since watchmen often deal with bad news, inspirers who speak positive words of encouragement into a watchman's life are vital.

INSPIRER

Inspirers move people by communicating hope through their words and deeds. Undeterred and undaunted by the odds and obstacles, these visionaries encourage people to find a path to victory. Although life can appear to be an advanced game of chess, they search for straightforward answers to complicated questions. "Keep it simple" is their mantra. Inspirers like to think big, see the future, and motivate people to act. It goes against their grain to standstill, not moving forward. Strategic by nature, they like connecting disparate dots and designing workable solutions to resolve pressing problems. Short-term benefits can be sacrificed for long-term gains in their mind.

> Inspirers move people by communicating hope through their words and deeds.

Mindful of their reputation, inspirers prefer to under-promise and over-deliver. Calculated risk-taking and careful decision-making reflect their leadership style. With eyes on the winners' circle, defeat is temporary and failure is not final. They are skilled at recovering from a fall and bouncing back from adversity. They get excited from discovering and sharing "lessons learned" from self-introspection or external observation. Ever ready to leave yesterday behind, they prefer looking through the windshield and not at the rear-view mirror. Today is a fresh new start and tomorrow is an opportunity to be better based on their optimistic outlook.

When walking in the Spirit, inspirers speak reassuring words during tests and trials. They bring affirmation and edification in the face of depression and oppression. They are positive—and not negative—regardless of the circumstances. Calm, cool, and collected, these people seek stability and order amid crisis and chaos. Love and life flow from their spirit. Words are their tools to help heal a broken heart or rebuild a low self-esteem. Adding value to people is their way of life.

In the absence of the Holy Spirit, inspirers can be covetous and lustful. Pride and arrogance can snare their foot time, and time, and time again. Loneliness and listlessness can be their weaknesses and hold onto them tight like a vise-grip. Feeling "lost" in life can be a hindrance to moving forward. Material things can take the place of God and usher them into idolatry. They can become obsessed with maintaining their image. They would do well to be hearers and doers of the Word of God. Challengers can sharpen inspirers and help them find the balance needed to succeed in life.

CHALLENGER

Challengers open up people to grow. They are used by God to release the potential He placed in mankind. They see what people can do— and be—despite real or perceived spiritual, mental, or physical limitations. They are growth specialists who do not accept excuses. They reject status quo thinking and the "woe is me" mentality. As a nutcracker splits open the shell of a seed, a challenger breaks through the hardness of a heart. Challengers are tools wielded by God to bring out the best in others. Whether they speak softly and carry a big stick or speak roughly and carry a small feather, these fearless folks are essential in helping many people realize their calling, equipping, and outcomes potential in Christ Jesus.

> Challengers open up people to grow.

Challengers are driven by a strong conviction to see hearts changed and lives transformed. Gentle engagement and intense confrontation are different routes to the same goal, nudging a person to reveal and remove what is holding them back in life. They desire people—especially those closest to them—to realize their fullest potential. In their mind, idleness brings death, industriousness brings life, and actions speak louder than words. They celebrate people who are productive and not lazy. They value concrete steps taken to address a matter and not piles of promises. "Be real with yourself" is the best counsel for personal development in their book. They stress being honest, not being deceitful, for someone to change and remain changed.

As messengers of God, challengers bring godly conviction with their words when led by the Holy Spirit. Passionate and forceful describes their usual manner of speech. Direct and definitive is their typical style of communication. Foolish folks will liken their chastisement to throwing sand in the eyes or pouring salt on wounds. Wise people will welcome their divine counsel like a cool breeze in summer or a warm wind in winter. Challengers can open blinded eyes by tearing the veil of deception, lies, and fraud.

However, challengers can be judgmental and controlling when operating outside of God. Anger and bitterness can spring forth if they walk by sight and not by faith. They can be sharp and harsh when frustrated. If not walking in love, they may have few friends, and relationships may be strained. They should regularly "look on the bright side." Inspirers can help challengers look at a glass as being half-full and not half-empty.

BUILDER

Builders bring security by creating structures or teaching concepts. One type of builder is a craftsman skilled to lay a physical foundation, design a solid structure, or erect a tangible edifice. Their creations can provide shelter from the elements, safety from the enemy, and space to gather before God. Another type of builder is a teacher gifted to impart a word of knowledge, convey a message of wisdom, or provide a key to under-

> Builders bring security by creating structures or teaching concepts.

standing. Their teachings can edify in different ways such as developing competence, building confidence, and fostering courage. Regardless of whether it is bonding metal to wood and making a physical structure, or connecting concepts to ideas and crafting a mental framework, builders are essential to facilitating environments where people can be safe and secure.

When builders flow in their divine calling, their creations or teachings are powerful and amazing. Disciplined, detailed, and precise, anointed builders bring the "wow" factor to the works of their hands and minds. They value feedback and welcome assistance in tackling projects, especially when the scale and scope is significant. They cultivate valuable relationships and collaborate well with strategic partners. They are task-oriented, methodical, and purposeful in what they do. Creativity, versatility, and flexibility characterize different phases of their work flow. Although their workshop may appear messy and disorganized, their finished work will be polished and awe-inspiring.

Outside of the Spirit, builders can be gullible and susceptible to deceptive offers. They can become angry and impatient when faced with limited time and finite resources. Seeking contentment and fulfillment apart from the Creator may result in them walking in delusion and blindness. They can be cold, calculating, and callous without the love of God in their heart. Faith in God and love for people remedies most of their challenges. They need to envision the result of their labor. Sowers can help builders see the fullness of their efforts by revealing the long-term implications of certain decisions.

WORSHIPER

Worshippers bring holiness by glorifying God with the sound of their voice or honoring Him through the work of their hands. Their humility and obedience moves the heart of God and influences multitudes. Purity, power, and passion are evident in their expressions of love and joy toward the Lord. Focused like a laser beam, worshippers channel their energy and effort into pleasing God. Whether the medium is through song, dance, or art, worshippers charge the atmosphere of the anointed with their words, actions, or works and bring glory unto God. Unrelenting in their pursuit of holiness and unapologetic for their faith, worshippers are the front lines of defense when people are attacked. They soothe the souls of the stricken and stir the hearts of the warriors. People are restored and ready to stand when worshippers walk in faith.

> Worshippers bring holiness by glorifying God with the sound of their voice or honoring Him through the work of their hands.

When worshippers worship in Spirit and in truth, the power of God is manifested. Mountains melt, distractions disappear, and forgiveness flows when they magnify God. Their praise unto God shatters shackles. Their dancing before God lightens hearts. Their art, celebrating God, warms souls. Acknowledging God, reflecting His magnificence, and honoring His presence are what worshippers love to do.

Without the Spirit of God, worshippers may fall into indiscretion and idolatry. Following false gods and serving unclean spirits are common traps many step into. Hypocrisy and debauchery may be their stumbling blocks if their hearts are far from God. Manipulation and deception may flow out of their spirit. They should remain sensitive to the Holy Spirit through prayer and fasting. Conquerors can help worshippers harness the confidence needed to be as impactful as possible.

SOWER

Sowers lay the groundwork for individuals to see and realize change in their lives. Planting seeds and revealing truth is their focus. Committed to learning about people and propelling them into greener pastures, sowers invest their time, talent, and treasure into developing others.

> Sowers lay the groundwork for individuals to see and realize change in their lives.

Desiring to see people emerge from present-day predicaments, they seek to win over hearts and minds through sound reasoning and self-sacrifice. Bold and brave with backbone, these motivated momentum-builders combine compelling rationale with penetrating insight to land their message. They are persuasive, persistent, and positive in their interactions and will go to great lengths to make a convincing case to their audience.

Sowers sold-out for God do not rest until the job is done. With unshakable faith and a mission-driven mindset, they open closed eyes through enlightened perspectives. Highly regarded and deeply respected, they capitalize on their credibility and urge people to turn toward the light. Able to grasp complicated concepts and explain them in simple terms, they are effective in marshaling the rationale to persuade diverse listeners to accept Christ. Realizing planted seeds precede planned harvests, they diligently and consistently lay out reasons why people should follow their doctrine. Through piercing logic and probing questions, they present facts and reveal truth that is undeniable.

Sowers seduced into compromising their standards become ineffective. Unbridled anger and arrogance may be on display if they do not have their way. Lack of conformity to established guidelines and lack of respect for predetermined procedures can result in confusion and chaos. Fear and hypocrisy can grip them and undermine their image and message. Walking in love always and being patient under pressure will enable them to continually bear good fruit. Builders can help sowers reap bumper crops from their seeds by helping them cultivate healthy and sustainable relationships.

JESUS WALKED IN HIS CALLING

Jesus walked in His calling. He fulfilled everything God wanted Him to fulfill. Christ left no stone unturned. He is our model and revealed the key to fulfilling our calling: humility and obedience. Jesus embodied all nine calling types and showed us how to please God. He bowed to the authority of the Father and did what He was sent to earth to do: offer life to the lost. He walked in faith, did not doubt his purpose, and stayed in

> Jesus embodied all nine calling types and showed us how to please God.

His lane. He was called to the lost sheep of the house of Israel and stuck to the divine plan.

Those who were not in that category came to Jesus (such as the persistent woman who sought her daughter's healing and was willing to eat crumbs from the master's table). Jesus did not search them out. This may be a hard truth to accept, but it is an important concept to grasp. It was the job of the Holy Spirit to bring the gospel to the rest of the world outside of Israel. This is why Jesus said He had to leave for the Holy Spirit to come upon the earth. The Holy Spirit facilitated the spread of the gospel beyond the borders of Israel. Why did it have to be this way? The Almighty God who created the universe and everything in it through Jesus Christ decided it was to be this way. This was His perfect plan before earth was birthed. The thoughts and ways of God are far beyond ours.

Jesus Christ was nailed to a wooden cross and murdered on a hill enabling everyone to be saved. Forgiveness for all sin was purchased through His shed blood. His death, burial, and resurrection enabled each and every person to be reconnected to God. Father God tasked the Holy Spirit to draw multitudes to Him due to the saving work of the blood of Christ. Disciples of Christ had to receive the Holy Spirit—and be empowered by the act of the Holy Spirit coming upon them—to go forth and minister the gospel. While Jesus was on earth, the disciples were sent to preach to the lost sheep of the house of Israel. After Jesus rose from the dead, the disciples were charged to bring the gospel to the rest of the world outside of Israel.

Jesus Christ—who was the walking Word of God anointed by the

Holy Spirit to minister—told the disciples *what* they were called to do, *where* they were called to do it, and *when* they were called to do it. The Word of God in conjunction with the Holy Spirit of God revealed to the people of God the *what, where,* and *when* of their calling. This is the case today as well. Through the Word and the Spirit, the people of God can find and fulfill their calling. Disciples of Christ were humble and obedient unto

> The Word of God in conjunction with the Holy Spirit of God revealed to the people of God the *what, where,* and *when* of their calling.

Jesus Christ and walked in their calling. Power and authority flowed through them and people were blessed in mighty ways.

The disciples knew their purpose and walked in it. They realized their calling, equipping, and outcomes potential in Christ. The disciples were not flawless superheroes who walked upon the earth; they were human beings with feelings and emotions that struggled with doubt and fear. At times, they lacked faith and failed to please God. Their true stories of trial and triumph, pain and joy, and lack and abundance are similar to the real-life stories of many Christians today. Despite their flaws and shortcomings, God called them to perform a work and used them as long as they were willing.

Today, followers of Christ must know what they were called to do and stick with the plan. Since Christ remained focused on what He was commissioned to do (ministering to the lost sheep of the house of Israel), it is imperative we do the same. Christ was humble and obedient before Father God. He demonstrated humility and obedience by walking along His designated path and not veering from it. If He can do it, so can we—for He promises we "can do all things" through Him (Philippians 4:13). He strengthens us to walk the walk and not just talk the talk. We are empowered to succeed over and over again if we know the Word of God and are led by the Holy Spirit.

Do not be deceived into thinking you can be in the will of God while not walking in your calling. It simply cannot happen, and any thought to the contrary is utter foolishness. When we stray from the path designed for us, we open the door to pride and invite calamity and catastrophe into our lives. We are left with little recourse than to hope calamity and catastrophe do not accept our invitation. If you are in this boat, turn your heart to Jesus, get on track, and be led by the Holy Spirit. God is awaiting your decision and is patient. Be convicted today to seek His face, find your place, and run your race.

WALK IN YOUR CALLING

Great things happen when you walk in your God-given calling. You step out of darkness and into the light. Disappointment dies and life thrives. Your spirit is sweet and your soul is satisfied. The Holy Word of God and the Holy Spirit of God will help you find and fulfill your calling. Let us pause here for a moment though and deal with a real issue: perception. For many people, the Word of God is nothing more than words on paper, and the Holy Spirit is just the name of some unseen mysterious thing. Now, it might seem puzzling and perplexing that the Word and

> Great things happen when you walk in your God-given calling.

the Spirit are keys to realizing your fullest potential in life. If you have a hard time seeing the Bible as more than a history book and the Holy Spirit as being more than a fable, I encourage you to change your perception. It will serve you well, now and into the future.

The Word of God can be found in the Bible, a God-inspired collection of writings from prophets, apostles, and others over several thousand years. Practical knowledge and sage wisdom for living on earth are found in it. The Word of God is more than ink on processed wood fibers. It is life and power and reveals the heart of man, and it prepares humanity for life after death:

> For the word of God is living and powerful, and sharper than any two-edged sword, piercing even to the division of soul and spirit, and of joints and marrow, and is a discerner of the thoughts and intents of the heart. (Hebrews 4:12 NKJV)

The Holy Spirit is the life force—or breath—of God. As you may recall, God breathed His breath into a lump of dust and gave it life thousands of years ago. The newly formed living being was called "man" and named Adam. Made in the image and likeness of God, Adam had the holy breath of God within his lungs. That breath enabled him to speak words and communicate with the Creator. Every descendant of Adam, including every human being on earth, has the same holy breath of God within his or her lungs.

> And the LORD God formed man of the dust of the ground, and breathed into his nostrils the breath

of life; and man became a living being. (Genesis 2:7 NKJV)

Although you cannot see your breath (the fog you witness when the moisture in your warm breath meets cool air does not count), you know you have it and it is not a mystery. Your breath is a measure of the Holy Spirit within you. Think about this: you must breathe to talk. This means you have to use the holy breath of God you received to speak. The holy breath of God within you is also known as your spirit. You are not the owner of your spirit, but a steward over it. You are a caretaker of the property of God, which is your spirit, until He takes it back.

> Or do you not know that your body is the temple of the Holy Spirit who is in you, whom you have from God, and you are not your own? (1 Corinthians 6:19 NKJV)

Obviously, you cannot walk in your God-given calling without God. Study the Bible and learn about Him. There are many different translated versions of the Bible. Pick one that works for you. I happen to use the New King James Version (NKJV) and the Amplified Bible, Classic Edition (AMPC) most frequently. Even though vocabulary and grammar might differ between various translations, the same Spirit is behind them all. The Holy Scripture contained in the Bible is from God and without error. It instructs in godliness and teaches the truth.

All Scripture is inspired by God and is useful to teach us what is true and to make us realize what is wrong in our lives. It corrects us when we are wrong and teaches us to do what is right. (2 Timothy 3:16 NLT)

Scripture tells us to be guided by the Holy Spirit of God. We will not walk in the sinful godless nature (the flesh) when we are humble before God and obey His Spirit's instructions. Guaranteed success follows those who follow the Spirit. This does not mean difficulties and hardships will not come. But God will deliver those who trust and follow Him out of every test and temptation. Trust Him. He will not forget you but will bless you abundantly.

So I say, let the Holy Spirit guide your lives. Then you won't be doing what your sinful nature craves. The sinful nature wants to do evil, which is just the opposite of what the Spirit wants. And the Spirit gives us desires that are the opposite of what the sinful nature desires. These two forces are constantly fighting each other, so you are not free to carry out your good intentions. (Galatians 5:16–17 NLT)

Walk in your calling and be led, guided, protected, surrounded, and empowered by the Holy Word of God and Holy Spirit of God. The power of the Word becomes your reward and the fruit of the Spirit becomes your reality

> Walk in your calling and be led, guided, protected, surrounded, and empowered by the Holy Word of God and Holy Spirit of God.

when you are committed to Christ and take the steps revealed to you. Realize the fruit of the Spirit in your life on a continual basis and you will experience the dominion and authority God originally intended for man to have on earth.

> But the Holy Spirit produces this kind of fruit in our lives: love, joy, peace, patience, kindness, goodness, faithfulness, gentleness, and self-control. There is no law against these things! (Galatians 5:22–23 NLT)

Look at the following benefits when you walk in your calling:

1. When you walk in your calling, love leads.

2. When you walk in your calling, joy dwells.

3. When you walk in your calling, peace prevails.

4. When you walk in your calling, patience manifests.

5. When you walk in your calling, kindness occurs.

6. When you walk in your calling, goodness grows.

7. When you walk in your calling, faithfulness flows.

8. When you walk in your calling, gentleness shows.

9. When you walk in your calling, self-control dominates.

LIVE YOUR CALLING AND NOT ANOTHER'S

A sure way to fail is to abandon (or neglect) your God-given calling and pursue a different calling. If you are called to deliver, then deliver. If you are called to conquer, then conquer. If you are called to worship, then worship. If you are called to inspire, then do not try to conquer. If you are called to challenge, then do not try to build. If you are called to watch, then do not try to comfort. To be clear, you are supposed to walk in love at all times. Also, it is true that people can have a strong secondary calling. However, your priority is to walk faithfully in your primary calling and not lose focus.

Remember, your core calling comes naturally to you and it can be easy to lightly esteem it because it may require little effort on your part to walk in it. Be consistent (and patient) in walking out your principal calling and be amazed at the results. You will see the things you—righteously and not lustfully—desire come to pass. Just stay in your assigned lane.

It can be tempting to see fruit and favor coming to people moving on another path. An inspirer can be jealous of the influence of a conqueror. A challenger can be envious at the success of an inspirer. A conqueror can be unsettled at the impressiveness of a challenger. However, it is foolish to think you can reap a great harvest on another field when you have not even succeeded in growing crops on your own land.

The seed you have is designed for the soil you possess. The calling God

> The seed you have is designed for the soil you possess.

gave you is like a seed specially designed to prosper in the soil He gave you. Your spirit, soul, and body are the three parts of the whole you, and they jointly constitute the soil where your calling is to take root, grow, and prosper. Be like the strong tree planted by the rivers of water whose leaf does not wither. Till your own soil and eat fruit from your own land. It will be refreshing and nourishing. Satisfaction guaranteed!

It is impossible to successfully walk on a path God did not design for you. Fish are not intended to survive out of water and birds are not designed to live underwater. Though some fish can pop out of the water and get back in and some birds can dive into water and come back out, those experiences are special circumstances and short lived. Prolonged exposure to air will kill a fish and too much time underwater will drown a bird. Pain is possible because failure is inevitable when a person strays from their God-given calling and tries to live in someone else's world.

> It is impossible to successfully walk on a path God did not design for you.

Why waste your time? One word explains it: covetousness. This is when you are bent on possessing something regardless of the cost. You want something so intensely that the ends justify the means. You are so consumed with claiming something right now that you refuse to be patient. As a result, you recklessly risk your name, reputation, and lifeblood—or that of another person. Covetousness is a sin that leads to destruction and death.

Desiring to possess something through a route you should not take will take you to the realm of the dead. Consider Eve as a primary example. She saw that fruit from the tree of the knowledge of good and evil was desirable to make one wise. She plucked it and ate it. She also gave some to Adam, and he ate it. What was the result of their sin? Their calling, equipping, and outcomes potential died, and so did they.

Did God not want Adam or Eve to receive knowledge of good and evil at some point in the future? I do not know. However, it is clear that God did not want them to obtain such knowledge by eating fruit from the tainted tree. God told them not to eat from that tree, but they disregarded the commandment and sealed their fate. The lustful desire to possess something through the wrong route resulted in an inglorious ending to two promising lives. Will the same be said of you? If you want a different outcome, stay on your path and seek God's counsel. He will show you how to walk right before Him and prosper.

PEACEFUL JOY

How can you expect to feel while walking in your calling? Peaceful joy is the answer. This is not a giddy excitement but a deep-seated satisfaction after successfully interacting with a person or carrying out a task in accordance with your purpose. You are recharged and refreshed by the experience and welcome future opportunities to engage people and projects.

> God designed you to fulfill a purpose.

There is a soothing hum on the inside as your spirit rejoices in being aligned with the will of God. In short, you are riding high and enjoy-ing your mountaintop experience above the clouds.

God designed you to fulfill a purpose. What He has called you to *do* is your path to peace and prosperity. Do not be concerned about how many times you have sinned and failed. God loves you uncondi-tionally and will not withdraw His calling upon your life.

> For the gifts and the calling of God are irrevocable.
> (Romans 11:29 NKJV)

CHAPTER 6

COMFORTER, DELIVERER, AND CONQUEROR

NOAH, JOSEPH, AND JOSHUA

COMFORTER

Comforters are called and equipped to bring peace and relief in connection with God-ordained agreements. Their calming nature soothes nerves and settles conflicts. They are often the go-to people to deal with intense and difficult situations. Noah was a comforter. His life should be an inspiration to those who struggle with spiritual identity. He knew who he was in God and where he stood. He was a man with divine vision and purpose. Noah heard and heeded the voice of God. He was humble and impacted the lives of billions of people.

BACKGROUND: WHO WAS NOAH?

God called Noah, who was in the tenth generation from Adam, to comfort people. He listened to God and was equipped with His grace, Word, and Spirit to restore the world. Violence had tainted the earth and wickedness was everywhere. God was displeased and decided to destroy mankind along with the beasts, bugs, and birds. The cursed earth needed cleansing, and God would use a devastating worldwide flood to accomplish it.

> So God said to Noah, "I have decided to destroy all living creatures, for they have filled the earth with violence. Yes, I will wipe them all out along with the earth!" (Genesis 6:13 NLT)

God used Noah, a righteous man living in a wicked and corrupt generation, to save mankind and creatures from utter destruction. Noah walked with God, and his family was spared due to grace.

However, God did not encapsulate them in an air bubble and float them in the sky during the flood. Noah was prompted by the Holy Spirit (spirit of faith) to do something clear, specific, and pioneering, which was to build a massive multi-level ark with rooms, a door, and a window. Armed with measurements from God, Noah constructed a three-story masterpiece to carry eight passengers (him, his wife, his three sons, and their wives) and two of every animal, insect, and winged creature. Add gathering food to feed people and creatures for over five months, and you had a major building project and rescue mission led by a trailblazing amateur.

So Noah did everything exactly as God had commanded him. (Genesis 6:22 NLT)

Noah was obedient and did what God commanded. After he built and coated the ship with pitch to withstand the rigors of catastrophic weather, floodwaters came and covered the entire earth. Mountaintops were swallowed up from gushing water springs and torrential downfall over forty days and forty nights. The ark traveled on the surface of the floodwaters and landed on a mountain as the waters receded. Noah sent out birds to explore and then took a look and saw dry land. The crew and cargo then left the ship and repopulated the planet. Post-flood, God equipped Noah with His Word again, blessing him and his sons, and commanded them to be fruitful and multiply.

> Noah was obedient and did what God commanded.

Noah accomplished what he was called to do. He comforted his family—and by extension, all of mankind—by doing the following three things: 1) making an ark to deliver both crew and cargo from total annihilation; 2) gathering food to nourish his family and the wildlife during the lengthy ark journey; and 3) receiving the blessing of God to replenish the entire earth. Noah's actions facilitated a great outcome, which was an enduring covenant established by God. God pledged to never again destroy the earth with floodwaters and set a rainbow in the clouds as the sign of the covenant. Noah accepted this agreement. As a result, he comforted his people and revived the earth through his righteousness and obedience.

MAKER

"Make yourself an ark of gopherwood; make rooms in the ark, and cover it inside and outside with pitch. And this is how you shall make it: the length of the ark shall be three hundred cubits, its width fifty cubits, and its height thirty cubits." (Genesis 6:14–15 NKJV)

God tasked Noah with the awesome responsibility of building a big boat to carry the seed of the earth. Without modern tools, digital imagery, or satellite photographs, this five-hundred-year-old father of three built a seafaring vessel capable of withstanding a multi-month voyage. Building the ark didn't require experience... only an obedient heart and willing hands.

> Building the ark didn't require experience... only an obedient heart and willing hands.

What amazing thing has God called you to construct? What special project has He instructed you to launch? What book has He inspired you to write? Perhaps you are uneducated, inexperienced, or unqualified based upon the world's standards. That does not matter if you have the Holy Spirit dwelling in you, and you are willing to die for Jesus—to surrender your life and accept His image. You are powerful and prosperous in Christ.

God will equip you, encourage you, and support you for the endeavor He designed for you. You are His plan, His craftsmanship, and His chosen vessel. Allow the Word of God to touch your heart and lighten the burden upon your shoulders, and accept God's unearned grace and favor. He built you to run a race no one else could run. He made you to live a life no one else could live. You are His first and best choice. Do not be deceived by the wisdom of the world, which is weak, dull, and defeated. You are blessed, anointed, and appointed to do exactly what He designed you to do. Pray, obey, and move forward with confidence. Trust in the Lord with all your heart and do not be moved by what detractors may say. God is truth.

GATHERER

"And you shall take for yourself of all food that is eaten, and you shall gather it to yourself; and it shall be food for you and for them." (Genesis 6:21 NKJV)

God instructed Noah to gather food for the journey. However, it was not just for him and his family but for the multitude of beasts and creatures in the boat as well. Any trip worth taking requires sustenance and nourishment to function, whether spiritual or natural food.

Before you embark on a path, gather the resources you and your companions need to live. Keep in mind that the goal is to thrive and not just survive along the way.

God is with you wherever you go and will even bring water from a rock if you stumble along the way and miss the mark. Do not fear the travel or fret the distance. God designed the path and equipped you to overcome obstacles along the way. Jesus is the great I AM, your strength and shield on the battlefield. Life is about choices and challenges. Choose the life God called you to live and avoid strife. Peace and stability are yours if you lay down your life for Christ. Gather various Scriptures for your situation, meditate on them, and communicate with the Lord. He will show you the path forward or the way out because He loves you.

RECEIVER

> So God blessed Noah and his sons, and said to them: "Be fruitful and multiply, and fill the earth." (Genesis 9:1 NKJV)

God commanded Noah and his sons Shem, Ham, and Japheth to reproduce and replenish the earth. These men were blessed, which means "empowered to succeed." Nothing could stand in their way except themselves. This was a turning point in the history of creation, when four men were called and equipped by God to do what other men could not do: bring life back to a devastated planet. Currently, the world's population is over seven (7) billion, and every person descended from these men.

Noah was a righteous man of faith. He was found worthy by God to be entrusted with the ark project. His three sons were with him and were blessed. The earth was filled, nations were birthed, and people of God multiplied. This is the way it ought to be. The righteous prosper and the world is blessed. God wants you to receive all He has in store for you. Walk in righteousness and obedience, and the glory of God will manifest in your life.

BE A PIONEER

Comforters are often pioneers. Has God called *you* to do something unprecedented? Did He tell *you* or lead *you* to marry a friend, have a baby, learn a language, launch a business, move a family, or buy a home? If you answered "yes" to these or similar promptings, the story of Noah hopefully inspired you to embrace ordained challenges and take action. God called you to do something unique and different. You were shaped in heaven and sent to earth for a reason. You were chosen to bless people and impact generations. Dreams and desires advancing His will for your life must come forth despite your weaknesses, inabilities, and insecurities. You are what He says you are, anointed and appointed to please Him. Trust God today and do what you have been called to do, even if it seems improbable or impossible.

> Trust God today and do what you have been called to do, even if it seems improbable or impossible.

Be a pioneer. It is in your nature because you already are! Think about it. You are the first and only you. There has not been—and shall not be—another person like you. You can do everything God has called you to do. Accept the tasks assigned to you, and plow forward with full confidence in the power of God. He cannot lose. Do not allow discouragement to defeat you. Do not permit detractors to derail you. I did, and it cost me. Is there music inside of you silenced by fear? Are there books within you blocked by laziness? Repent, seek the face of God, and move forward. I did, and it straightened me out. It was hard and humbling, but necessary and good. What are you waiting for? Does a catastrophe need to occur? Does an angel need to appear before you? An amazing life is yours for the taking. Amend your ways and prosper. You were called and equipped to make a difference.

NOAH: CALLING, EQUIPPING, AND OUTCOME

Calling (Comforter):

> Lamech lived one hundred and eighty-two years, and had a son. And he called his name Noah, saying, "This one will comfort us concerning our work and the toil of our hands, because of the ground which the LORD has cursed." (Genesis 5:28–29 NKJV)

Equipping (Grace of God upon Noah):

> But Noah found grace in the eyes of the LORD. This is the genealogy of Noah. Noah was a just man, perfect in his generations. Noah walked with God. (Genesis 6:8–9 NKJV)

Equipping (Word of God Spoken to Noah):

> And God said to Noah, "The end of all flesh has come before Me, for the earth is filled with violence through them; and behold, I will destroy them with the earth.

Make yourself an ark of gopherwood; make rooms in the ark, and cover it inside and outside with pitch." (Genesis 6:13–14 NKJV)

Equipping (Spirit of God Prompting Noah):

[Prompted] by faith Noah, being forewarned by God concerning events of which as yet there was no visible sign, took heed and diligently and reverently constructed and prepared an ark for the deliverance of his own family. By this [his faith which relied on God] he passed judgment and sentence on the world's unbelief and became an heir and possessor of righteousness (that relation of being right into which God puts the person who has faith). (Hebrews 11:7 AMPC)

Equipping (Word of God Spoken over Noah):

So God blessed Noah and his sons, and said to them: "Be fruitful and multiply, and fill the earth." (Genesis 9:1 NKJV)

Outcome (No-Flood Covenant):

"Thus I establish My covenant with you: Never again shall all flesh be cut off by the waters of the flood; never again shall there be a flood to destroy the earth." And God said: "This is the sign of the covenant which I make between Me and you, and every living creature that is with you, for perpetual generations: I set My rainbow in the cloud, and it shall be for the sign of the covenant between Me and the earth." (Genesis 9:11–13 NJKV)

DELIVERER

Deliverers bring people out of bondage and facilitate their freedom. They are God's tools to right wrongs and level playing fields. With focused minds and passionate hearts, deliverers visualize and pursue the end game. Their calling is often clarified amid calamity. Joseph is a primary example. Persecuted, framed, and forgotten, he developed a heart for those in dire need. Unbowed in spirit despite years of incarceration, God elevated him to deliver the embryonic nation of Israel out of the clutches

> Deliverers bring people out of bondage and facilitate their freedom.

of a devastating famine. When given the opportunity to exact revenge on his brothers who persecuted him, he rejected bitterness and chose love. Joseph's testimony of true forgiveness in the face of emotional anguish is a stark reminder to not harbor hard feelings toward anyone. Anger and hatred in your heart and mind will enslave you more than shackles and chains on your hands and feet.

BACKGROUND: WHO WAS JOSEPH?

> Jacob loved Joseph more than any of his other children
> because Joseph had been born to him in his old age.
> So one day Jacob had a special gift made for Joseph—a
> beautiful robe. (Genesis 37:3 NLT)

Joseph, one of the twelve sons of Jacob (later renamed Israel), was his father's favorite child. Born when his dad was old, Joseph enjoyed special status and wore a beautiful coat his father made. However, after he revealed dreams (where his parents and brothers bowed down to him), his father rebuked him and his brothers despised him. Life grew more difficult for the favorite son as things took a turn for the worse. Jealousy and hatred consumed his brothers' hearts, and they conspired to kill him when the opportunity arose. Saved by the merciful heart of his eldest brother, Reuben, Joseph was spared an untimely death—for he needed to fulfill the God-given calling on his life. He was destined to deliver his relatives out of a severe worldwide famine engulfing the family homestead in Canaan, the land promised by God to his father Jacob, grandfather Isaac, and great-grandfather Abraham. Abraham (formerly known as Abram) was a direct descendant of Shem, a son of Noah.

> Then Midianite traders passed by; so the brothers
> pulled Joseph up and lifted him out of the pit, and
> sold him to the Ishmaelites for twenty shekels of silver.
> And they took Joseph to Egypt. (Genesis 37:28 NKJV)

Though he escaped murder at the hands of his own flesh and blood, Joseph was stripped of his ornate coat and tossed into an empty pit without water. Considering his brother Judah's appeal to not shed his blood and instead sell him into slavery, his brothers pulled him out of the dry hole and traded him for silver. The Ishmaelites, who purchased Joseph, brought him to Egypt and sold him to Potiphar, a high-ranking official in the royal guard of Pharaoh. Although Joseph was a slave, God was with him and prospered him. The blessing of God was evident and resulted in Joseph finding favor in his master's eyes. Potiphar made Joseph the overseer of his house.

> "There is no one greater in this house than I, nor has he kept back anything from me but you, because you are his wife. How then can I do this great wickedness, and sin against God?" (Genesis 39:9 NKJV)

Even after being framed by Potiphar's wife and thrown into prison, God never left Joseph's side. He gave Joseph favor with the jailer, who put him in charge of the prisoners and their affairs. Joseph trusted in God and walked by faith. With the spirit of discernment upon him, he interpreted the dreams of Pharaoh's head butler and head baker who were jailed after offending Pharaoh. Joseph said the butler would be restored to his position in three days, but the baker would be executed. Knowing liberation was forthcoming for Pharaoh's cupbearer, Joseph asked him to petition his release before the king. After the baker lost his life and the butler regained his freedom, Joseph was forgotten about and languished in the dungeon for a full two years. However, he did not allow himself to become bitter.

> And Pharaoh said to Joseph, "I have had a dream, and
> there is no one who can interpret it. But I have heard
> it said of you that you can understand a dream, to in-
> terpret it." So Joseph answered Pharaoh, saying, "It is
> not in me; God will give Pharaoh an answer of peace."
> (Genesis 41:15–16 NKJV)

Disturbed by a dream his magicians and wise men could not understand, Pharaoh sought someone who could explain the dream. The
butler remembered Joseph and recommended him. This imprisoned
Israelite—with God's favor upon him—interpreted Pharaoh's dream
and was elevated to rule over all Egypt. Joseph used this delegated
authority to bring his brothers, his father, and dozens of other family
members to Goshen, the land of safety within Egypt. Full of love,
Joseph forgave his brothers for their betrayal. He chose not to be arrogant and angry, but opted instead to be humble and compassionate.
Evacuating the family from famine-stricken Canaan to the safety of
Goshen in Egypt resulted in their deliverance from the physical bondage of hunger. Walking in forgiveness toward his brothers freed them
from the mental bondage of guilt. Only God could design such a
beautiful outcome—his family's deliverance and his brothers' freedom.

Joseph was a righteous and honest man who shared his God-given
dreams, refused to lie with Potiphar's wife, secured Egypt during an
oppressive global famine, saved his family members' lives, and forgave
his once mean-spirited brothers. Joseph is a great model for the mod-

ern-day Christian suffering persecution from family members, close associates, or friends. He did not give up on life and neither should you. Regardless of whether Joseph was a dreamer, prisoner, or ruler, one thing remained the same: he trusted in God and remained humble.

> Regardless of whether Joseph was a dreamer, prisoner, or ruler, one thing remained the same: he trusted in God and remained humble.

DREAMER

And he told it to his father [as well as] his brethren. But his father rebuked him and said to him, What is the meaning of this dream that you have dreamed? Shall I and your mother and your brothers actually come to bow down ourselves to the earth and do homage to you? Joseph's brothers envied him and were jealous of him, but his father observed the saying and pondered over it. (Genesis 37:10–11 AMPC)

Joseph's dream did not sit well with his father and brothers. He faced a consequence at his brothers' hands: captivity. His punishment? He was stripped of his colorful coat and tossed into a pit, sold for twenty pieces of silver to a band of Arabian traders, taken into Egypt, and resold to Potiphar. What a trip! A teenage boy whose father desperately loved him found himself in hot water with his brothers over dreams he was excited to tell.

Have you experienced people attacking you after you shared your hopes and dreams? Has the spirit of jealousy come upon your family members or risen among your friends when you have opened your heart and communicated God-given visions? Do not fret or fear. Such a story played itself out thousands of years ago. The same God who called Joseph out of Canaan and into Egypt to save the Israelites has placed purposes and passions within you for His divine plan. Rejoice when Spirit-filled dreams excite you and people persecute you over them. Pray for the salvation and deliverance of those family members, friends, or strangers and trust God to deal justly with them through His Holy Spirit.

PRISONER

> And Joseph's master took him and put him in the prison, a place where the state prisoners were confined; so he was there in the prison. But the Lord was with Joseph, and showed him mercy and loving-kindness and gave him favor in the sight of the warden of the prison. (Genesis 39:20–21 AMPC)

Framed! Potiphar's wife accused Joseph of trying to lie with her when she was the one trying to snare him. She lied and he was jailed. Innocent, indicted, and imprisoned. What a raw deal! He did nothing wrong to deserve such punishment. He was persecuted for being a righteous man of God.

Have you been arrested, convicted, and sentenced for a crime you did not commit? Repent now for any hatred or unforgiveness you may be carrying against the accuser, prosecutor, judge, or jury that played a role in stealing your freedom. Have any family members, friends, associates, or colleagues blamed you for something you did not do? Confess any grudge you are nursing and move on. Regardless of whether your bondage is literal or metaphorical, know that Jesus is the truth and the truth has already set you free. Trust in Christ to turn your situation around, release you from captivity, and place you on higher ground. He did it for Joseph, and can do it for you. Worship God from your place of pain and allow His love to heal your heart.

> Worship God from your place of pain and allow His love to heal your heart.

RULER

And Pharaoh said to his servants, Can we find this man's equal, a man in whom is the spirit of God? And Pharaoh said to Joseph, Forasmuch as [your] God has shown you all this, there is nobody as intelligent and discreet and understanding and wise as you are. You shall have charge over my house, and all my people shall be governed according to your word [with reverence, submission, and obedience]. Only in matters of the throne will I be greater than you are. Then Pharaoh

said to Joseph, See, I have set you over all the land of
Egypt. (Genesis 41:38–41 AMPC)

Redeemed! Joseph went from the prison to the palace in an in-
stant. Pharaoh gave him his signet ring, plus fine linen, a gold chain,
and—most importantly—authority. No man could lift his hand or
foot in Egypt without Joseph's consent. What an amazing level of
responsibility thrust upon a thirty-year-old former inmate! God looks
upon the heart and not the situation. Joseph did not become bitter or
dejected. He was patient and ready when the opportunity for emanci-
pation presented itself.

Where are you today? Whether in a concrete cell block or a spiritual dungeon, you can learn from Joseph and set your heart on heavenly and not earthly things. Jesus is heavenly as He was not from earth.
He stepped down from glory, wrapped Himself in flesh, and lived
among us. Jesus is our Savior and
Shepherd. Look upon Him, remember
the cross, and seek His face daily. Peace
is found when the heart is sound.

> Peace is found when the
> heart is sound.

> "Now therefore, do not be afraid; I will provide for
> you and your little ones." And he comforted them and
> spoke kindly to them. (Genesis 50:21 NKJV)

Joseph the ruler cemented his power when he walked in love toward his brothers. He forgave them for the evil they did to him. Jesus
asked God to forgive those who crucified him.

What are you waiting for? There is no good reason to walk in unforgiveness, but there is a profound reason to walk in love, which is God. God is love. Walk with God. Walk in love. Forgive the person who wronged you and open a door of righteousness in your life. Did your spouse abandon you? Did your best friend betray you? Did someone take credit at work for something you did? Have you been raped or molested? Have you been beaten or tortured? Have you been stabbed or shot? Regardless of the bad deed, you must forgive the person and pray for them. Pray for their salvation. Pray for their deliverance. Pray for their peace. Pray for their family. Pray for them to forgive themselves. It may be hard, but it is godly. Your love will bear fruit.

Have you been the bully? Have you been the liar? Have you been the murderer? Repent (turn away from your sin) and forgive yourself. If you do not forgive yourself, you are in sin. Sin is missing the mark. Sin separates us from God and destroys us. Sin is a cause of sickness and poisons the heart and mind. Forgiveness is a type of medicine and promotes healing and well-being. It brings peace and prosperity. Forgiveness flows from a heart of love, which is where God, Jesus, and the Holy Spirit dwell.

> If you do not forgive yourself, you are in sin.

BE A BROTHER

A brother is a male bonded to someone due to an intimate, unique, or special relationship. A sister is a female connected to a person in like manner. Take stock of your close relationships with family, friends, and other people, and ask yourself if you are being the best brother or sister you can be. Measure yourself with God's unconditional love. Be honest and do not hide the truth for it shall set you free. God gave us families for a reason. Whether the connection is through lineage or marriage, race or ethnicity, school or sports, recreation or rehabilitation, friendship or employment, worship or fellowship, there are people close to you.

How do you treat those with whom you have meaningful relationships? Are you walking in integrity? Conduct a self-assessment and ask tough questions. Consider honesty. Have you lied to a family member before? I know I have. Confessing faults and asking for forgiveness is hard for the flesh but soothing for the soul. Although lies to others are bad, lies to oneself are worse, quite often. Guilt, shame, and condemnation flow from self-deception. Have you forgiven yourself lately? Love yourself. Walk away from the prison you built. Appreciate life. Welcome God's love into your heart. Love people.

Have you been wronged before? Have you been hated? Have you been rebuked? Have you been envied? Have you been betrayed? Have you been sold? Have you been trafficked? Have you been accused? Have you been imprisoned? Have you been forgotten? If you answered "yes" to any of the above, or have had something similar happen, then the story of Joseph should be one of comfort and encouragement.

> Guilt, shame, and condemnation flow from self-deception.

Forgiveness is an act of love. It can

heal hurt hearts and release guilty minds. God called you to walk in love toward everyone, especially to those who oppose you. It is not your job to judge and hold a grudge. God said He would bless those who bless His people, and curse those who curse His people. Pray your adversaries seek the face of God. He desires all men to be saved, and so should you.

JOSEPH: CALLING, EQUIPPING, AND OUTCOMES

Calling (Deliverer):

"And God sent me before you to preserve a posterity for you in the earth, and to save your lives by a great deliverance. So now it was not you who sent me here, but God; and He has made me a father to Pharaoh, and lord of all his house, and a ruler throughout all the land of Egypt." (Genesis 45:7–8 NKJV)

Equipping (Favor of God Given to Joseph):

But the LORD was with Joseph and showed him mercy, and He gave him favor in the sight of the keeper of the prison. (Genesis 39:21 NKJV)

Equipping (Spirit of God Within Joseph):

And Pharaoh said to his servants, "Can we find such a one as this, a man in whom is the Spirit of God?" (Genesis 41:38 NKJV)

Outcome (House of Jacob Evacuated to Egypt):

All the persons who went with Jacob to Egypt, who came from his body, besides Jacob's sons' wives, were sixty-six persons in all. And the sons of Joseph who were born to him in Egypt were two persons. All the persons of the house of Jacob who went to Egypt were seventy. (Genesis 46:26–27 NKJV)

Outcome (Joseph Forgives His Brothers):

When Joseph's brothers saw that their father was dead, they said, "Perhaps Joseph will hate us, and may actually repay us for all the evil which we did to him." So they sent messengers to Joseph, saying, "Before your father died he commanded, saying, 'Thus you shall say to Joseph: "I beg you, please forgive the trespass of your brothers and their sin; for they did evil to you."'" Now, please, forgive the trespass of the servants of the God of your father." And Joseph wept when they spoke to him. Then his brothers also went and fell down before his face, and they said, "Behold, we are your servants."

Joseph said to them, "Do not be afraid, for am I in the place of God? But as for you, you meant evil against me; but God meant it for good, in order to bring it about as it is this day, to save many people alive. Now therefore, do not be afraid; I will provide for you and your little ones." And he comforted them and spoke kindly to them. (Genesis 50:15–21 NKJV)

CONQUEROR

Conquerors are called to win big and bring victory through raw displays of power and might. Whether it is physical strength, intellectual prowess, or spiritual dominion, true conquerors have mastered the virtue of self-control and use their talents as tools. No challenge is too great and no mountain too high for these gifted achievers. They reject fear and doubt and embrace faith and determination. Invaluable to have on board when times get tough, conquerors are the ultimate team leaders and team players, when focused.

> Conquerors are called to win big and bring victory through raw displays of power and might.

Joshua, Moses' successor, was called to conquer and lead the nation of Israel into the promised land. Anointed by his mentor, Moses, to carry the torch for a new generation, Joshua accomplished God's will. Obstacles were overcome and enemies were defeated. Peace was possessed and stability was secured. The children of God were in a position to prosper in their own land as a result of Joshua the conqueror.

BACKGROUND: WHO WAS JOSHUA?

> And Moses said to Joshua, "Choose us some men and
> go out, fight with Amalek. Tomorrow I will stand on
> the top of the hill with the rod of God in my hand."
> (Exodus 17:9 NKJV)

Joshua, though a young man, was Moses' assistant and a warrior. He led military campaigns against enemy forces and possessed discernment and courage, which are key leadership traits. He breaks onto the scene almost midway into the book of Exodus as the person Moses entrusted to choose warriors to fight Amalek, an archenemy of the Israelites. He defeated Amalek with the edge of the sword—which was great training for future battles. He would soon lead Israel across the Jordan River and fight for possession of the promised land (Canaan). His victories were secured because God was with him wherever he went.

> But Joshua the son of Nun and Caleb the son of
> Jephunneh, who were among those who had spied out
> the land, tore their clothes; and they spoke to all the
> congregation of the children of Israel, saying: "The
> land we passed through to spy out is an exceedingly
> good land." (Numbers 14:6–7 NKJV)

After twelve Israeli spies came back from scoping out the land of Canaan, all of them—except for Joshua and Caleb—said the Israelites could not conquer the land. They saw giants residing there and could not conceive how to win. Joshua and Caleb were fearless fighters with firm confidence in the ability of God to manifest His will. They were unconcerned with what they saw and focused instead on what God said, which was that the land was theirs for the taking. In their eyes, the power of God was sufficient to defeat the inhabitants of Canaan. Joshua and Caleb both walked by faith and not by sight. They did not doubt the ability of God to make good on His word, which was that the land of Canaan was their inheritance.

> After the death of Moses the servant of the LORD, it came to pass that the LORD spoke to Joshua the son of Nun, Moses' assistant, saying: "Moses My servant is dead. Now therefore, arise, go over this Jordan, you and all this people, to the land which I am giving to them—the children of Israel." (Joshua 1:1–2 NKJV)

Charged by God to secure the land He promised to the children of Israel, Joshua was now responsible for finishing the deliverance work Joseph began and Moses continued. God used Joseph to bring the house of Jacob from Canaan to Egypt due to famine in the land. The Israelites had greener pastures in the Egyptian city of Goshen and remained there for four hundred years. Oppression and cruelty at the hands of the Egyptians fell down hard upon the children of Israel, and they suffered intense mental and physical abuse.

God raised up Moses to bring them out of Egypt and into the land where they would take root and prosper. Moses, who was adopted by Pharaoh's daughter, refused to remain in the palace and joined his brethren in the camp. Commissioned by God to demonstrate mighty signs and miracles before Pharaoh, Moses secured the release of the people and led them out of Egypt and to the border of Canaan. After Moses viewed the majesty of the land flowing with milk and honey, he died on a mountaintop and was received by God. God selected Joshua to assume leadership over the nation and conquer the giants in the promised land. Joshua, who was equipped with the Word and Spirit of God, realized great outcomes because he obeyed authority, had faith in God, and was humble.

> Joshua, who was equipped with the Word and Spirit of God, realized great outcomes because he obeyed authority, had faith in God, and was humble.

OBEY AUTHORITY

So Joshua did as Moses said to him, and fought with Amalek. And Moses, Aaron, and Hur went up to the top of the hill. (Exodus 17:10 NKJV)

The kingdom of heaven and the kingdoms of earth operate on the principle of authority. There is a leader responsible for casting vision and providing direction. The people who support the leader are tasked with carrying out the assignments. Heaven and earth would collapse if they were not based on authority. Respect for authority is paramount to God, for all authority derives from Him. To rebel against authority on earth is to rebel against authority in heaven. His will is to be done on earth as it is in heaven. The devil was evicted from heaven because he rebelled against God's authority. Don't repeat the same mistake; rather, be like Joshua who obeyed Moses and did as he was instructed. Joshua fought against the Amalekites and won.

FAITH IN GOD

"If the LORD delights in us, then He will bring us into this land and give it to us, 'a land which flows with milk and honey.' Only do not rebel against the LORD, nor fear the people of the land, for they are our bread; their protection has departed from them, and the LORD is with us. Do not fear them." (Numbers 14:8–9 NKJV)

Faith in God is all you need to succeed. God delights in people who have faith. Faith enables you to please God and manifest His power. Do not undermine your faith by walking in fear. Please note I am *not* talking here about fear as in the "fear of God." To fear God means to deeply respect, honor, and revere Him. The bad feeling that results from the threat or presence of danger is a different fear—a fear that comes when you do *not* respect, honor, and revere God. Fear is the enemy of the soul. It robs people of rights and privileges available to them due to being made in His image and likeness. Faith and fear are polar opposites. Faith is good and fear is bad. Faith is light and fear is darkness. Faith is positive and fear is negative. Love reveals whether you are operating in faith or fear. Faith operates through love and fear operates in

> Fear is the enemy of the soul.

the absence of love. Joshua and Caleb loved God. They had faith in God and did not walk in fear. They urged their brethren to not rebel against God by walking in fear of the people in Canaan. Joshua and Caleb knew God.

HUMILITY

And it came to pass, when Joshua was by Jericho, that he lifted his eyes and looked, and behold, a Man stood opposite him with His sword drawn in His hand. And Joshua went to Him and said to Him, "Are You for us or for our adversaries?" So He said, "No, but as Commander of the army of the LORD I have now come." And Joshua fell on his face to the earth and worshiped, and said to Him, "What does my Lord say to His servant?" Then the Commander of the LORD's army said to Joshua, "Take your sandal off your foot, for the place where you stand is holy." And Joshua did so. (Joshua 5:13–15 NKJV)

There is little God will not do for someone who walks in humility and obedience. We all need to have the mind of Jesus Christ. Christ was humble and obedient and sacrificed His life for all of us to fulfill the sovereign will of God. Glory and greatness awaits the person who lives for God and not self. It is incumbent upon all mankind to embrace the gift of humility and resort to no other tactic than obedience. Obedience opens the door to the supernatural realm and releases the power of God on your behalf. Raise your level of obedience.

Authority is activated when obedience is elevated. Darkness is penetrated when obedience is elevated. Sin is decimated when obedience is elevated. Humility coupled with obedience is a powerful and unbeatable combination. Cancer and all forms of sickness and disease flee in the face of a humble and obedient child of God full of love and forgiveness. Understand the authority you have in Christ Jesus over your health and wealth. Financial prosperity comes to those who are humble, obedient, and pure in heart.

> Authority is activated when obedience is elevated.

Joshua was called to lead Israel and was equipped with the spirit of wisdom, which is the Holy Spirit, to complete the deliverance process Joseph started and Moses furthered. Joshua brought his people across the Jordan River into Canaan, defeated their enemies, and claimed the land promised to them by God. These impressive outcomes were realized because obedience, love, and humility flowed out of the heart of the conqueror. Joshua was a real man of God and walked with God. He trusted in the Lord and knew God was always with him.

BE A VISIONARY

How do you become a powerful and compassionate leader trusted by God? Establish your own relationship with the Almighty and find out what He wants you to do. Have His vision for your life and walk in it. He knows your beginning, your end, and all points in between. God called and ordained you to fulfill a unique role on earth. He created

you through Jesus Christ and has empowered you through the Holy Spirit to
go above and beyond your self-imposed
limitations and comfort zone.

> God called and ordained you to fulfill a unique role on earth.

God envisioned you. God fashioned you. God released you. Embrace these realities. Your life is not your own. You were conceived with a purpose and mandate. Pray for knowledge, wisdom, and understanding. Worship God and praise His power. Be righteous and walk your ordered path. Live rooted and grounded in God's love. He is with you just as He was with Joshua. You cannot fail with God. Seek Him. See Him. Serve Him. He has given you victory over every challenge. He has made a way for your escape. He has conquered your enemies.

What is your vision of yourself? Do you see yourself as a winner or loser? You cannot rise above your self-image. You were made in the image and likeness of God. If you do not see yourself in Him, you cannot see Him in you and failure is inevitable. Without vision, you perish (Proverbs 29:18). Be not deceived by Satan who comes with worldly wisdom. I consented to his rationale many times over the years because I had a weak relationship with my Creator. When I draw closer to God, the wickedness in my life becomes clearer and the love of God in my life becomes stronger.

Abide in the Lord and resist temptation. Let God expose the sin in your life. Repent and move on. This will allow the beautiful vision God has for your life to manifest. The Lord is magnificent, magnanimous, and merciful. See that He is on your side! Joshua did and realized the vision God had for His people, which was dwelling in the land flowing with milk and honey.

JOSHUA: CALLING, EQUIPPING, AND OUTCOME

Calling (Conqueror):

Then Moses called Joshua and said to him in the sight of all Israel, "Be strong and of good courage, for you must go with this people to the land which the LORD has sworn to their fathers to give them, and you shall cause them to inherit it." (Deuteronomy 31:7 NKJV)

Equipping (Spirit of God):

Now Joshua the son of Nun was full of the spirit of wisdom, for Moses had laid his hands on him; so the children of Israel heeded him, and did as the LORD had commanded Moses. (Deuteronomy 34:9 NKJV)

Outcome (Promised Land Possessed):

So the LORD gave to Israel all the land of which He had sworn to give to their fathers, and they took possession of it and dwelt in it. The LORD gave them rest all around, according to all that He had sworn to their fathers. And not a man of all their enemies stood against them; the LORD delivered all their enemies into their hand. Not a word failed of any good thing which the LORD had spoken to the house of Israel. All came to pass. (Joshua 21:43–45 NKJV)

CHAPTER 7

WATCHMAN, INSPIRER, AND CHALLENGER

EZEKIEL, DAVID, AND JOHN THE BAPTIST

WATCHMAN

Watchmen warn people about what is on the horizon. Because strategies and resources are often deployed as a result of their forecasts, the watchman's calling carries a heavy responsibility. As a result, many watchmen seek to shape the future by understanding the past and present and developing actionable strategies. Many people spend years—sometimes even entire careers—studying data and analyzing facts in hopes of uncovering trends and identifying patterns. Regardless of whether it is developing plans to win soccer games, outperform financial markets, or secure military victories, researching past and present performance to influence future events keeps many watchmen engaged. Accuracy is vital and there can be significant consequences for being wrong. Depending on the situation, lives could be lost if a watchman is off. The Spirit of God is the most important asset for any watchman because only God knows the past, present, and future.

BACKGROUND: WHO WAS EZEKIEL?

On the fifth day of the month, which was in the fifth year of King Jehoiachin's captivity, the word of the LORD came expressly to Ezekiel the priest, the son of Buzi, in the land of the Chaldeans by the river Chebar; and the hand of the LORD was there upon him. (Ezekiel 1:2–3 AMPC)

Ezekiel was a person just like you and me. God called him to play a role in the lives of many people. He was gifted with the privilege of seeing the future and tasked with the responsibility of communicating it to the children of Israel. Through His Word and Spirit, God declares His divine plans and purposes and reveals things that are mysterious and hidden. Ezekiel was equipped with the Word and Spirit to speak truth to a nation. Sometimes the truth hurts and is hard to accept. Prideful and disobedient people reject the exposure of their deeds. Unfortunately, they do not understand that mercy for their faults is found in the truth. Humble and obedient people welcome the refining power of revelation. Fortunately, they understand that acknowledging their weaknesses opens the door to grace. How can you overcome challenges in your life if you refuse to open your eyes, mind, and heart to the truth?

> Through His Word and Spirit, God declares His divine plans and purposes and reveals things that are mysterious and hidden.

And He said to me, "Son of man, stand on your feet,
and I will speak to you." (Ezekiel 2:1 NKJV)

God set apart Ezekiel to be a watchman. His job was to hear the Word of God and warn the people. Ezekiel was filled with the Holy Spirit and had visions revealing the spirit realm and the future. God wanted him to speak the straight truth and not be moved if the people did not receive it.

The same God who made Ezekiel made you and me. We have the same capacity to hear directly from God and see into the invisible spirit world through the Holy Spirit.

So I prophesied as I was commanded; and as I prophesied, there was a [thundering] noise and behold, a shaking and trembling and a rattling, and the bones came together, bone to its bone. (Ezekiel 37:7 AMPC)

Ezekiel accepted God. He heard His words and communicated them as instructed. God performed the words He spoke through Ezekiel, laid His hand upon him, and released His power. Power was demonstrated when God told Ezekiel to speak life into dry human bones. Ezekiel did as he was commanded. The bones came together, flesh appeared, and the breath of life entered. God worked through a man to raise an army from the dead. Now, that was a great outcome!

VINDICATION OF THE LORD

Son of man, behold, they of the house of Israel say, The vision that [Ezekiel] sees is for many days to come, and he prophesies of the times that are far off. Therefore say to them, Thus says the LORD God: There shall none of My words be deferred any more, but the word which I have spoken shall be performed, says the LORD God. (Ezekiel 12:27–28 AMPC)

Ezekiel had no need to be concerned about whether what he said would come to pass. He had God's words in his heart and just needed to speak as directed. The Holy Spirit of God led Ezekiel and facilitated his face-to-face experiences with the Holy One. Ezekiel only needed to walk in his calling. He did not need to try and figure out why God called him and how God was going to do what He said he would do. The elders of Israel discounted the currency of Ezekiel's words by saying they were for a latter day. However, God was clear that Ezekiel was right and the elders of Israel were wrong, vindicating Ezekiel. Although Ezekiel was the messenger, he did not need to try and prove the veracity of the words spoken by God. It was God's role, not Ezekiel's, to bring the words of God to pass. Too often people believe they must make something happen when they speak the words of God. That is erroneous thinking. Wisdom says do what you have been instructed, and leave the outcome to God.

> Although Ezekiel was the messenger, he did not need to try and prove the veracity of the words spoken by God.

HAND OF THE LORD

The hand of the LORD was upon me, and He brought me out in the Spirit of the Lord and set me down in the midst of the valley; and it was full of bones. And He caused me to pass round about among them, and behold, there were very many [human bones] in the open valley or plain, and behold, they were very dry. (Ezekiel 37:1–2 AMPC)

God uses His hand to display His power on earth. When the hand of the Lord is "for" someone, miracles happen. But when the hand of the Lord is "against" someone, judgment happens. It is preferable to be on the miracle side of the equation, like Ezekiel. The hand of the Lord transported him in the spirit to a physical location with lots of dry bones. His job was to speak life into those dead bones. Has God ever dispatched you into a seemingly dead situation to bring words of faith, hope, and love? Do not be dismayed if God sends you to speak to someone who dislikes you or is known for persecuting people like you. The hand of the Lord might be against that person to reveal and root out their rebellion. You might be the messenger assigned to bring the word of life or the warning of death to their doorstep. Do not fear the people you must engage. Do not be moved by any choice words they may hurl in your direction. Do not faint in their presence and fail to deliver the message. If God selected you to bring the truth to someone, welcome the assignment and carry out the task.

POWER OF THE LORD

And He said to me, Son of man, can these bones live?
And I answered, O Lord God, You know! Again He
said to me, Prophesy to these bones and say to them,
O you dry bones, hear the word of the LORD. Thus
says the Lord God to these bones: Behold, I will cause
breath and spirit to enter you, and you shall live.
(Ezekiel 37:3–5 AMPC)

God has life-giving power and it is released through the words of
man. What you speak can bring life to a dead situation. Position yourself to unlock the awesome power of God. All it takes is humility,
obedience, faith, and a willingness to be used by God. He has no fa-
vorites. God loved the entire world and sent Jesus to die for everyone.
That included every despotic dictator who destroyed life. The worst
thing someone can do is reject Jesus Christ, the Holy Spirit, and Father
God. Turning your back on God, who
is three-in-one, and not repenting will
deliver you to death, the enemy's prison. People who proclaim the Prince of
Peace as Lord and Savior with a genuine
heart possess life and the power of God.

> God has life-giving
> power and it is released
> through the words
> of man.

Christ is the power of God, and those who are His are joint-heirs with
Him. This power-sharing agreement is special and unique. Value the
strength made available to you through the blood of Jesus. His birth,
life, death, burial, and resurrection were preordained by God to deliver
you from darkness and bring you into the light. The purpose of the

power of God residing within you is to free you from sin and bind you to the Lord. Be bound!

BE A SPOKESPERSON

Have you been tasked to speak on behalf of someone? Have you been hired to articulate the views of an organization? Being the "voice" of a person or entity is an important role. Why? Words are impactful and consequential. Remember, God spoke the world in which we live into existence. Words matter. You build up or break down with words. You project strength or demonstrate weakness with words. You create life or produce death with words. Words are relevant. Words are powerful. Words are critical. Do not underestimate the weight of words.

Do you speak positive or negative words? Words either move you forward or move you backward. Words are seeds, and you reap what you sow. Be careful what you plant because harvest time *will* come. What type of crop do you want? You are your own spokesperson. Your words frame your world. Change your life by changing your words. God has provided a life script to follow in the person of Jesus Christ. Have an intimate relationship with the Lord and Savior and put His words into your mouth.

> Change your life by changing your words.

Many years ago, I asked God to pay for graduate school. I had been accepted to a great program and wanted to attend. One day I received two pieces of mail. A student loan approval was in one envelope and a graduate school fellowship application was in the other. The fellowship paid for graduate school in exchange for serving as a US diplomat after graduation. I was thrilled! I knew what the *perfect* will of God was in my spirit. There was not a shadow of a doubt. I stood on Scripture and declared the fellowship was mine in the name of Jesus Christ. It was not a vain exercise in mind science. I released my faith and possessed my blessing. To put action behind my faith, I ripped up the student loan approval and threw it into the trash. Debt was not necessary since I knew I had the fellowship, by faith.

Afterward, I applied for the fellowship and went through a lengthy vetting process. Several months later, I was in graduate school with the fellowship in hand and a dream job on the horizon. I spoke my future into existence by faith and backed up my words with concrete actions. God wants His people to prosper. Do you believe this statement is true or false? It is up to you. Do you want to be a victor or a victim? It is your choice. Do you desire relationship or religion? That is your call.

Ezekiel was a prophet who spoke truth to power. He was led by the Holy Spirit and said what God instructed. Ezekiel chose to have a relationship with the Creator. He could have made a different decision. Fortunately, he owned his outcome and fulfilled the will of God. Ezekiel was a spokesperson for God. He listened to what God told him to share and repeated it to the people God intended to receive the message: the children of God. We should take a page from his book and walk in a similar manner.

Let us listen to what the Lord says and speak as He directs. If you are married, expect God to give you knowledge to share with your spouse. If you are a parent, expect God to give you wisdom to pass on to your children. If you are a coach, expect God to give you encouragement (also known as a pep talk) to share with your athletes. Be a spokesperson for God inside and outside your home. The power of God will be released through your words.

EZEKIEL: CALLING, EQUIPPING, AND OUTCOME

Calling (Watchman):

"Son of man, I have appointed you as a watchman to the house of Israel; whenever you hear a word from My mouth, warn them from Me." (Ezekiel 3:17 AMP)

Equipping (Spirit of God):

And the Spirit entered into me when He spoke to me and set me upon my feet, and I heard Him speaking to me. And He said to me, I send you, son of man, to the children of Israel, two rebellious nations that have rebelled against Me. They and their fathers have transgressed against Me even to this very day. (Ezekiel 2:2–3 AMPC)

Outcome (Dry Bones Came Alive):

So I prophesied as He commanded me, and the breath and spirit came into [the bones], and they lived and stood up upon their feet, an exceedingly great host. (Ezekiel 37:10 AMPC)

INSPIRER

Inspirers bring hope. Jesus is hope. Therefore, inspirers bring Jesus. Inspirers move people when they display the character of Christ. Jesus was humble, obedient, faithful, and powerful. He acknowledged God's authority and obeyed Him. He had faith in Father God and released His power. Inspirers influence others to the greatest degree when they themselves walk with Jesus. This is because their ability to motivate people is wrapped up in their ability to demonstrate the love of Christ. Love is the ultimate currency of success for an inspirer because love is the basis for all hope. It is not by natural strength that one inspires but by the Spirit of the Lord. Even if inspirational people may be weak in their flesh, they can be strong in their heart. The flesh is the outward appearance, but the heart is a person's inward identity.

> Inspirers bring hope.

BACKGROUND: WHO WAS DAVID?

> Samuel also said to Saul, "The LORD sent me to anoint you king over His people, over Israel. Now therefore, heed the voice of the words of the LORD. Thus says the LORD of hosts: 'I will punish Amalek for what he did to Israel, how he ambushed him on the way when he came up from Egypt.'" (1 Samuel 15:1–2 NKJV)

For many years after Joshua died, the children of Israel were ruled by people called judges. God established the judges, who administered the nation. The prophet Samuel was one of the last judges, and he appointed his sons to be judges when he was old. The people did not want his wayward children to serve in such capacity and demanded a king to rule over them, like other nations. God did not want His people to adopt a model used by the world because He sought to govern Israel directly. But they desired to be like other nations and thus rejected God as sovereign leader. Nonetheless, God mercifully granted their wish and instructed Samuel to anoint Saul king of Israel. Saul's reign ended when he disobeyed God's command: he failed to destroy all the Amalekites and their livestock. Acting on his own accord, Saul spared the Amalekite king, Agag, and saved the choicest animals. Amalekites were sinners, and King Agag made women childless through his ruthlessness. The people and their king were wicked. Saul's pride and lust drove him to defy God. For his faithlessness, God rejected him as king over Israel. In his place, God anointed David, the youngest of eight sons of Jesse the Bethlehemite.

> Then Saul said to Samuel, "I have sinned, for I have transgressed the commandment of the LORD and your words, because I feared the people and obeyed their voice." (1 Samuel 15:24 NKJV)

Saul had two problems. The first was an issue most people face at one point in life: lack of love toward God. Saul loved himself more than God. This led to his second problem, which was selfishness. Saul lived for himself. Man was created to serve. If you are not serving God, then you are serving yourself. When you live for yourself and not for God, you derive your value and importance by what others say about you—but this is backward. God created you and called you out of your mother's womb, and you should thus receive your identity and worth by what your Creator says about you. Saul's heart was tainted because he served himself and not God. David replaced Saul as king because he had a heart that desired God first. The heart of God is love. Mercy and compassion flow from a loving heart. God seeks people who love Him and mankind.

> When you live for yourself and not for God, you derive your value and importance by what others say about you—but this is backward.

> Now the LORD said to Samuel, "How long will you mourn for Saul, seeing I have rejected him from reigning over Israel? Fill your horn with oil, and go; I am sending you to Jesse the Bethlehemite. For I have provided Myself a king among his sons."
> (1 Samuel 16:1 NKJV)

David was not the people's choice, like Saul. Rather, he was God's choice. Born to a man with many sons, he was the youngest of the bunch. Young David was a keeper of sheep and walked with courage and confidence. Called to be a king before he was born, he learned how to lead and fight from shepherding sheep in the pasture. He defended the flock against predators and was strong and reliable. To David, a fierce enemy was a threat to be neutralized. Unwavering in the presence of danger, this future ruler cut his teeth taking down wild animals. He fought against a bear and lion and won. David was a mighty man of valor who was anointed by God through the prophet Samuel to be king of Israel.

The Lord dispatched Samuel, with a measure of anointing oil, to visit Jesse and pronounce the Word of God over David. He ruled over Judah for seven years and over all Israel for thirty-three years. Although the people celebrated him for killing Goliath and defeating tens of thousands of people, he was also known for being a merciful man who inspired King Saul to admit his wrongdoing. Self-control is more powerful than military might. Master your emotions and thoughts and see the love of God flow out of your heart. Walking in love activates your faith and releases the unmeasurable power of God. Let love reign, and you will be a person after God's own heart.

SELF-CONTROL

Then he said to David: "You are more righteous than I; for you have rewarded me with good, whereas I have rewarded you with evil. And you have shown this day how you have dealt well with me; for when the LORD delivered me into your hand, you did not kill me. For if a man finds his enemy, will he let him get away safely? Therefore may the LORD reward you with good for what you have done to me this day. And now I know indeed that you shall surely be king, and that the kingdom of Israel shall be established in your hand." (1 Samuel 24:17–20 NKJV)

David was an inspirer because he showed restraint, or self-control. David spared Saul when it was within his power to kill him, and this restraint inspired Saul to admit his sin and acknowledge the will of God: David's appointment as king of Israel. Mercy is when you do not receive what you deserve. Saul deserved death because he sought to kill David for no justifiable reason. David knew Saul's death would not be by his hands and so showed him mercy. Saul was the anointed of God and David could not lay a hand on him. David respected, revered, and honored God to such an extent that he respected, revered, and honored the man God anointed. Though Saul disobeyed God and had the kingdom ripped away from him, the same God who anointed Saul also anointed David. David valued the anointer, the anointing, and the anointed! David's heart was pure, undefiled, and merciful, which is why David was a man after the heart of God.

> David was an inspirer because he showed restraint, or self-control.

> David valued the anointer, the anointing, and the anointed!

REVERENCE

David said furthermore, "As the LORD lives, the LORD shall strike him, or his day shall come to die, or he shall go out to battle and perish. The LORD forbid that I should stretch out my hand against the LORD's anointed. But please, take now the spear and the jug of water that are by his head, and let us go." (1 Samuel 26:10–11 NKJV)

Upset that the kingdom of Israel was torn away from him and given to David, jealous Saul attempted to murder David multiple times. Saul knew the Lord left him and chose David. Although David was anointed to be the next king, he revered the anointing of God upon Saul and refused to harm him. In contrast, Saul knew David was anointed to be his successor but did not honor the anointing of God upon David. Saul sought to fatally harm David. David respected God, but Saul did not. That was the bottom-line difference between the two men. Although they were both anointed to be king of Israel, they each handled their God-ordained responsibility differently. The state of the heart determines the outcome of the person. God placed His Holy Spirit upon Saul and gave him a new heart (1 Samuel 10:6-11). Unfortunately, Saul did not retain the pure heart given to him by God. He walked in pride and greed and ceased to flow in the Holy Spirit. Conversely, David walked with a pure heart after the Holy Spirit came upon him, and he obeyed God (1 Samuel 16:13). Although both were anointed to be king of Israel, only one held the office in a manner pleasing unto God. Be like David.

MERCY

"Is this not David, of whom they sang to one another in dances, saying: 'Saul has slain his thousands, And David his ten thousands'?" (1 Samuel 29:5 NKJV)

You may question whether David was truly merciful since he slew tens of thousands of people with the edge of the sword. How could a man with blood on his hands have a heart pleasing God? Press the pause button, and look at what resulted in Saul losing the kingdom. God instructed Saul, through the prophet Samuel, to destroy everyone and everything during the conquest of the Amalekites. Though such an order may seem harsh and excessive through our modern-day lens, it was the sovereign will of God to remove every trace of those wicked people from the earth. Look at the past. Because of the wickedness of humanity, God destroyed everyone on earth—except for Noah and his family—by flood. Noah was righteous and found favor with God. He and his family were spared and blessed. Look at the future. Christ will judge everyone at the end of the age and all the wicked will be cast into the Lake of Fire and destroyed (Revelation 20:12-15). The righteous will not suffer such a fate and live with God. God does nothing without a purpose. God wanted the Amalekites eliminated for a good reason: wickedness. Saul's choice to not destroy all the Amalekites was an act of rebellion and disobedience, and it's for this act of defiance that God tore the kingdom of Israel away from him.

BE A SPARK

What happens when you show mercy and forgiveness to a person who hates you or threatens your life? This is not a trick question. The answer is simple. A spark is created when you love the unlovely. Friction is generated when the love in your gentle heart strikes against the coarse surface of a hardened heart. Sparks fly when the friction releases energy. The sparks are sparks of love. Hopefully, a fire will ignite in the ungodly person's heart, and they will turn from their sins and toward the Lord.

The prophet Jeremiah likened the Word of God in his heart to fire contained within his bones (Jeremiah 20:9). Jeremiah grew tired of restraining the Word and had to release it, regardless of harsh words and terrible threats from critics. He could not be afraid of what people would say or do because of speaking the Word of God. Jeremiah had a job to do and could not allow a spirit of fear to come upon him and inhibit his purpose.

Have you ever had a time in your life when you knew God gave you something to say and it felt like a ball of fire churning in your belly? I did. Many years ago my then-future wife Jonnel and I visited a wonderful Christian couple, and we had a spirited prayer session. God gave me a word to share, but I was afraid to speak. While I was quiet and waiting for the moment to pass, the lady of the house turned to me and said do not be afraid to share what God told you to say. I froze! She read my mail and exposed my fear. After the shock wore off, I realized I should not restrain the Word when it is like a fire in my belly looking for a way out. Giving voice to a word of knowledge, wisdom, or understanding you are supposed to speak can pave the way for the power of God to flow.

> Giving voice to a word of knowledge, wisdom, or understanding you are supposed to speak can pave the way for the power of God to flow.

When you speak the Word of God, things happen in their proper season.

Do not be surprised if the time is quite short or very long. God has an appointed season for everything under heaven. When David faced Goliath, he spoke what God gave him to speak and told the giant he was going to kill him. David said his defeat would send a message to the whole world that there was a God in Israel. He declared that the battle was not his, but the Lord's. The time between David's declaration and Goliath's death was probably brief, perhaps only a few minutes. The power of God was demonstrated when David slew the giant by landing a stone from a slingshot right between his eyes. God backed up the words He gave David to speak. Why? David spoke the words at the proper time from a heart filled with faith in God. He was a man after God's own heart. The God-ordained words David spoke brought divine power onto the scene, which overcame Goliath and sparked courage and confidence in the hearts of others. The men of Israel rallied and defeated the Philistines after David slew Goliath by the Spirit of the Lord. David inspired people by his words and actions. Be a spark and inspire someone today.

DAVID: CALLING, EQUIPPING, AND OUTCOME

Calling (Inspirer):

> Then Saul said, "I have sinned. Return, my son David. For I will harm you no more, because my life was precious in your eyes this day. Indeed I have played the fool and erred exceedingly." And David answered and

said, "Here is the king's spear. Let one of the young men come over and get it. May the Lord repay every man for his righteousness and his faithfulness; for the LORD delivered you into my hand today, but I would not stretch out my hand against the LORD's anointed." (1 Samuel 26:21–23 NKJV)

Equipping (Spirit of the Lord):

So he sent and brought him in. Now he was ruddy, with bright eyes, and good-looking. And the LORD said, "Arise, anoint him; for this is the one!" Then Samuel took the horn of oil and anointed him in the midst of his brothers; and the Spirit of the LORD came upon David from that day forward. So Samuel arose and went to Ramah. (1 Samuel 16:12–13 NKJV)

Outcome (A Blessing):

Then Saul said to David, "May you be blessed, my son David! You shall both do great things and also still prevail." So David went on his way, and Saul returned to his place. (1 Samuel 26:25 NKJV)

CHALLENGER

Challengers are growth experts. They know how to water seeds and stimulate development. Ever desiring to bring out the best in people, they invest their time, talent, and treasure into winning hearts, minds, and souls. Whether their points are landed with an iron fist or a velvet hammer, they engage with gusto and grit. Challengers are a rare breed of people whose confidence can be confused with arrogance. Strong-willed, steadfast, and secure, they breathe life into dead situations and project light into darkness. Focused on continuous growth, they poke and prod until an impression is left. When faced with hardened hearts and skeptical minds, they press their rationale with passion and power. No giant is too big and no mountain is too high for challengers with purified hearts. Why? They know failure is not an option as God is on their side. They love a good challenge and a hungry soul. Regardless of whether their approach is coarse or smooth, challengers leave indelible marks on the lives they touch.

> Challengers are growth experts.

BACKGROUND: WHO WAS JOHN THE BAPTIST?

"Behold, I send My messenger, And he will prepare the way before Me. And the LORD, whom you seek, Will suddenly come to His temple, Even the Messenger of the covenant, In whom you delight. Behold, He is coming," Says the LORD of hosts. (Malachi 3:1 NKJV)

John the Baptist was the prophesied messenger anointed to pave the way for the Lord Jesus Christ. Set apart for this solemn purpose, this gifted and talented man was called to shake up the status quo by challenging people to embrace God. John was designed and destined to perform a specific assignment at a specific point in time. No force above, on, or under the earth could stop the plan of God. John was tasked with urging the children of Israel to confess their sins and be baptized with water. He declared that the kingdom of God was at hand. He called people to admit their wrongdoing, which would open the door for humility and obedience to become rooted in the heart. God was ready to do miraculous things through Jesus Christ and needed people to have faith to receive the blessings. Being humble and obedient enables the spirit of faith, which is the Holy Spirit, to flow like a river. Healing and restoration emanates from faith.

> But the angel said to him, "Do not be afraid, Zacharias, for your prayer is heard; and your wife Elizabeth will bear you a son, and you shall call his name John. And you will have joy and gladness, and many will rejoice at his birth." (Luke 1:13–14 NKJV)

John the Baptist's father was a priest named Zacharias. He and his wife, Elizabeth, were righteous people. They were humble and obedient before God and desired a child. However, the likelihood of them conceiving a child was slim, for she was barren—and they were both elderly. Fortunately, Zacharias was a committed husband who prayed for his wife to have a son. God heard his prayer and granted his request. Furthermore, God said the name of the boy would be John.

The birth of baby John was no accident. It was the preplanned, predetermined, and preordained will of God. God envisioned John walking and talking on the earth long before Adam and Eve were even on the scene. Did you know everyone born on earth was in God's heart and mind before the foundation of the earth was even laid? Everything about God has been and always will be purposeful and meaningful. There has never been anything vain or void about Him. You were part of God's vision of creation and born with a purpose, just like John the Baptist.

> For he will be great and distinguished in the sight of the Lord; and will never drink wine or liquor, and he will be filled with and empowered to act by the Holy Spirit while still in his mother's womb. He will turn many of the sons of Israel back [from sin] to [love and serve] the Lord their God. (Luke 1:15–16 AMP)

John the Baptist was destined to be great in God's eyes. He did not have to hope or pray for it. His spiritual DNA was already coded for greatness. Even if man did not see John as great, that did not matter. God saw his greatness, and that was all the validation he needed. John neither sought nor required acceptance from flesh and blood. His desire was to please God and not man. Called to live a strict lifestyle centered on loyalty to the Lord, John refrained from drinking wine and dwelt in the wilderness. Equipped with the Holy Spirit while still in the womb, he was empowered to preach the gospel and proclaim Christ. John was determined and committed to carry out his divine purpose. With a fiery and firm spirit, he pressed people to repent for

their sins and believe in God. Multitudes
of people followed the Lord as a result of
his faithfulness toward God and His
forthrightness toward men. He was led by

> John was determined
> and committed to carry
> out his divine purpose.

the Holy Spirit and challenged many Israelites to love and serve the
Lord. John the Baptist fulfilled his calling.

REPENT

In those days John the Baptist appeared, preaching
in the Wilderness of Judea [along the western side of
the Dead Sea] and saying, "Repent [change your inner
self—your old way of thinking, regret past sins, live
your life in a way that proves repentance; seek God's
purpose for your life], for the kingdom of heaven is at
hand." (Matthew 3:1–2 AMP)

Repent for the kingdom of heaven is near! This was the clarion
call of John the Baptist, the greatest man to walk the earth prior to
the Lord Jesus Christ. John spoke plainly. He was bold, direct, and
passionate. John understood the importance of repentance, which was
key to opening the door to eternal life. Repentance was accomplished
when past sins were confessed, and old ways were changed. Jesus was
coming soon and sought to find love, hope, and faith on earth. Those
who were truly remorseful about their wrongdoing and walked away
from a sinful life were prepared to receive the Lord Jesus. Those who
were not defied the Lord and marked their souls for condemnation.

You should be like the people who loved God more than themselves and gave their lives over to Him. Do not be like people who loved themselves more than God and did not turn their lives over to Him. Like everyone else in the world, you were born in sin and fell short of the glory of God. Do not be fooled into thinking you do not need to repent. Your spirit will be renewed when you confess past sins and change old thinking. Repentance has been—and continues to be—the path to peace, prosperity, and purpose.

COMMIT

> This is the one who was mentioned by the prophet Isaiah when he said, "The voice of one shouting in the wilderness, 'Prepare the road for the Lord, Make His highways straight (level, direct)!'" Now this same John had clothing made of camel's hair and a [wide] leather band around his waist; and his food was locusts and wild honey. (Matthew 3:3–4 AMP)

Commitment is a hard word for many people to grasp and accept because it requires folks to make decisions and stick with them. Follow-through and accountability are required to bring commitments to pass. The best thing you can do in life, living for the Lord, requires commitment. Salvation is not a flash-in-the-pan experience. Rather, it is an ongoing relationship. Commitment requires long-term thinking. You must look beyond the seconds, minutes, and hours of your day and look toward the weeks, months, and years of your life. Like a marathon, life requires patience, endurance, and steadfastness. God spoke about John the Baptist through the prophet Isaiah hundreds of years before John was conceived and born. He made a public commitment to bring John forth

> You must look beyond the seconds, minutes, and hours of your day and look toward the weeks, months, and years of your life.

when He prompted Isaiah to make the declaration. John's life was not a snap decision God made on the fly. He thought about what He wanted John to do and laid out his life, from beginning to end, prior to his physical manifestation on earth. God stood by His plan and held Himself accountable to fulfill it.

FULFILL

> At that time Jerusalem was going out to him, and all Judea and all the district around the Jordan; and they were being baptized by him in the Jordan River, as they confessed their sins. (Matthew 3:5–6 AMP)

Fulfillment is a beautiful word. It brings good things to mind such as joy, peace, and satisfaction. Your heart may even flood with excitement, love, and happiness when a desire is fulfilled. The most contentment you could ever experience in life is from fulfilling your calling in Jesus Christ. God designed your life and incubated you in your mother's womb until the day you needed to be separated. He called every person to love Him and give their life to Him. He called each person to *do* something and *be* something pleasing unto Him. You did

> After knowing Him, your quest in life should be to find and fulfill your calling.

not create your spirit, mind, or body. God did. He created the breath of life in your lungs, the tissue in your brain, and the flesh on your bones. Why? You were born to fulfill a purpose. After knowing Him, your quest in life should be to find and fulfill your calling. John the Baptist was born to proclaim the kingdom of heaven, urge sinners to repent, and baptize people with water. He found and fulfilled his calling. He ran his race and finished it. Be challenged by his faithfulness and follow suit.

BE DISCIPLINED

John the Baptist lived an intentional life. He focused his energy on doing what God called him to *do* and being what God called Him to *be*. He challenged people to admit the error of their ways and was a prophet who declared the kingdom of God. Now, many people have good intentions and desire to do and become certain things in life. However, the chasm between intentions and results is crossed by the

> Now, many people have good intentions and desire to do and become certain things in life. However, the chasm between intentions and results is crossed by the bridge of discipline.

bridge of discipline. I rejected it for many years because it involved sacrifice. Foolishness led me to believe I could succeed in life by only riding the favor of God. I was wrong. Favor does not yield success without discipline. God can send great things your way all day long, but you will not be able to handle them properly without discipline. If you do not believe me, think about your life (or the life of someone else) and look at what happened when the boat of favor set sail in a sea of laziness. Unnecessary problems or trip termination may have occurred. Mishandled favor can lead to unintended failure.

Discipline is needed to reap the fullness of God's favor and have true success. Do not be deceived into thinking you can fly and prosper without it. Reality will take hold at some point, and you will be grounded. The question is whether you will crash and burn or land and live. The price of discipline is humility and obedience. You must sacrifice worldly ways of thinking, speaking, and doing and embrace godly ways of thinking, speaking, and doing. Repent and turn to God. Be filled with His Word and Holy Spirit. Be filled with His grace and mercy. Be filled with His faith and love. Discipline will flow when you fill yourself with the right stuff. I realized this truth later in life. Trying to be disciplined in my own strength was never sustainable. I ran myself ragged and opened the door to self-imposed shame and condemnation. Walking by the Spirit of God and following His plan always brings me to the place of real success and fulfillment. You are responsible for being a good steward over your own life. When you love God and give your life to Him, the will to live comes and the desire for discipline arrives. Embrace it! God is disciplined, and He wants us to be like Him because discipline strengthens the spirit, mind, and body and enables us to enjoy the life He called us

> Walking by the Spirit of God and following His plan always brings me to the place of real success and fulfillment.

to lead. Although it may feel uncomfortable, discipline is necessary to find and fulfill our calling in Christ Jesus.

JOHN THE BAPTIST: CALLING, EQUIPPING, AND OUTCOME

Calling (Challenger):

> "And he will turn many of the children of Israel to the Lord their God." (Luke 1:16 NKJV)

Equipping (Spirit of God):

> "For he will be great in the sight of the Lord, and shall drink neither wine nor strong drink. He will also be filled with the Holy Spirit, even from his mother's womb." (Luke 1:15 NKJV)

Outcome (Baptized Believers):

> Then Jerusalem, all Judea, and all the region around the Jordan went out to him and were baptized by him in the Jordan, confessing their sins. (Matthew 3:5–6 NKJV)

CHAPTER 8

BUILDER, WORSHIPER, AND SOWER

NEHEMIAH, BEZALEL, AND PAUL THE APOSTLE

BUILDER

Builders are essential to the establishment and success of any community. They are needed to build new things or rebuild damaged things. They facilitate safety, security, and prosperity with the energy of their hearts, minds, and hands. Creativity is their primary tool and commitment is their primary strength. Builders find innovative solutions to difficult problems and stay on task until the job gets done. When Spirit-led, no challenge is too great and no barrier is too big. Focused and fearless, these people are extensions of the hands of God. Strong and determined, they are impressive individuals who leave lasting impressions.

BACKGROUND: WHO WAS NEHEMIAH?

And they said to me, "The survivors who are left from the captivity in the province are there in great distress and reproach. The wall of Jerusalem is also broken down, and its gates are burned with fire." (Nehemiah 1:3 NKJV)

A man on a mission is an apt description of this builder who lived several hundred years before Christ was born. Nehemiah was a cupbearer in the court of King Artaxerxes, which meant he served the king his wine. He was deeply saddened by the pain and suffering of his people back in Jerusalem and desired to be with them and rebuild the wall of Jerusalem. Nehemiah was closely knit to his brethren, and he grieved over their distress. He could not bear to have abundance in the palace while his people had lack in the field. His heart was fixed on helping his people.

So it was, when I heard these words, that I sat down and wept, and mourned for many days; I was fasting and praying before the God of heaven. (Nehemiah 1:4 NKJV)

> A devout man of God, Nehemiah turned to the Lord when his heart was broken over the misery facing his people.

A devout man of God, Nehemiah turned to the Lord when his heart was broken over the misery facing his people. Pay close attention to how he responded to the situation. He did not get angry. He did not become vengeful. He did not become bitter. Nehemiah chose to humble himself before God and seek His face through fasting and prayer. He obeyed the Holy Spirit's prompting within him. Nehemiah knew the Lord was the best—and only—way to deliver his people from their tortuous trial and tribulation.

> Then the king said to me, "What do you request?" So
> I prayed to the God of heaven. And I said to the king,
> "If it pleases the king, and if your servant has found
> favor in your sight, I ask that you send me to Judah,
> to the city of my fathers' tombs, that I may rebuild it."
> (Nehemiah 2:4–5 NKJV)

Prayer was central to Nehemiah's life. A prayer warrior who valued intimacy with the Lord, he turned to his Creator for guidance and direction. After the king he served asked him what he requested, Nehemiah prayed first before responding. Once he received the answer within his heart, he spoke. Mindful of his position within the palace, he prefaced his request with words of honor and respect for the king. Nehemiah then delivered his "ask" with clarity and specificity.

Prayer was central to Nehemiah's life.

> Then the king said to me (the queen also sitting beside
> him), "How long will your journey be? And when will
> you return?" So it pleased the king to send me; and I
> set him a time. (Nehemiah 2:6 NKJV)

With his queen at his side, the king granted Nehemiah's request and was pleased to send him to Jerusalem. Oftentimes, the very thing you request of God requires another human being to do something. As a servant in the king's court, Nehemiah did not have the right to just walk out of the palace and help his people in Jerusalem. He had to first ask for permission from his earthly master, King Artaxerxes.

> When we demonstrate our commitment to doing things in a manner pleasing unto God, resources become available and great things happen.

There is a rich lesson of humility in this situation. Nehemiah needed to work through man to realize the will of God for the children of Israel in Jerusalem. This is consistent with the order of God and of His kingdom. When we demonstrate our commitment to doing things in a manner pleasing unto God, resources become available and great things happen.

> Furthermore I said to the king, "If it pleases the king, let letters be given to me for the governors of the region beyond the River, that they must permit me to pass through till I come to Judah, and a letter to Asaph the keeper of the king's forest, that he must give me timber to make beams for the gates of the citadel which pertains to the temple, for the city wall, and for the house that I will occupy." And the king granted them to me according to the good hand of my God upon me. (Nehemiah 2:7–8 NKJV)

To rebuild the wall of Jerusalem, Nehemiah needed authorization to pass through multiple jurisdictions and secure building materials. The king granted him letters to travel and secure wood. When we pray with sincerity, God hears our requests and gives us guidance. His instructions may require us to be humble and obedient before man. God did not design us to be isolated beings who follow Him and disregard others. He called us to be in community with His created beings. Nehemiah received the letters he needed to get the job done. God is not a magician who performs tricks with smoke and mirrors. He is a loving, heavenly Father who wants the best for all of us. Do not expect God to snap His fingers and eliminate your problems. However, expect God to show you how to work through your challenges. The hand of God was upon Nehemiah (this was another way of saying the Holy Spirit was upon him). Nehemiah knew that the king granted him the letters he needed as a result of the Holy Spirit. Allow God to give you favor among people and resources through people. He is pleased when His people prosper.

> So the wall was finished on the twenty-fifth day of Elul, in fifty-two days. And it happened, when all our enemies heard of it, and all the nations around us saw these things, that they were very disheartened in their own eyes; for they perceived that this work was done by our God. (Nehemiah 6:15–16 NKJV)

Mission accomplished. Nehemiah led the campaign to rebuild Jerusalem's walls. Despite taunts and threats from enemies all around, this visionary leader rallied the people to believe in themselves and accomplish a great feat. Unmoved by the daunting task of rebuilding a city wall under the threat of war, Nehemiah inspired the leaders and the people to pray and trust in God. They complied and finished the task in the presence of their enemies. God worked through Nehemiah to demonstrate His power to all the nations surrounding Jerusalem.

HUMBLE

> The one and only answer to every catastrophe, every calamity, and every circumstance is Jesus.

What do you do when horrible news breaks your heart? What do you do when the worst-case scenario happens? What do you do when reality reduces you to tears? There is only one thing you can do to see you through to the other side: trust in the Lord. The one and only answer to every catastrophe, every calamity, and every circumstance is Jesus. Thrust yourself upon His altar of grace. Sacrifice your pride, preference, and pedigree, and pray. Humility is the road to strength, power, and deliverance. Nehemiah humbled himself before Almighty God and prayed. The Lord responded. The people were empowered. The wall was rebuilt.

OBEDIENT

Disobedience is an act of pride. Failing to do what God has commanded you to do is not good. People reap what they sow. Bad fruit comes from bad seed. God cannot be mocked. How do you expect people to heed your words when you do not heed His words? How do you expect people to show you respect when you do not show Him respect? How do you expect people to love you when you do not love Him? Keep your life simple by obeying God. Complicate your life by disobeying God. It is your choice. Choose wisely. Nehemiah did and an entire city was blessed.

FOCUSED

Distraction is the enemy of the good. It takes people off course and compromises missions. It results in costly losses and unintended consequences. It results in real problems and unrealized goals. Many well-designed plans have dissolved in seas of distraction. What is the solution to this unfortunate reality plaguing many people?

Focus.

Keep your mind on the task set before you, and do not give up. Remain committed to your calling, and do not let go. Stay aligned with your assignment, and do not go astray. Like Nehemiah, you were placed upon this earth to make something happen. He did not lose sight of the job he was called to do and neither should you.

BE A FOUNDATION

A foundation is reliable, durable, and strong. Jesus Christ is the firm foundation upon which our lives are built upon. Without Him, we are weak, unstable, and unable to prosper. Jesus is the author and finisher of our faith. This means he is our beginning, our ending, and everything in between. We cannot even breathe without His grace within and upon us. Christ is the cornerstone of all creation. Through Him, every planet and everything in the cosmos was created. Nothing has existed—or will exist—without Christ. Nothing you can conceive will have any lasting value without Him. Make Christ the center of any endeavor, enterprise, or engagement and you'll experience great success. Victory is always attainable and sustainable through the Lord.

> Make Christ the center of any endeavor, enterprise, or engagement and you'll experience great success.

Be like Jesus and be a firm foundation by being rooted and grounded in love. Jesus was motivated by love in everything He did. This was His testimony from the dateless past and shall be His testimony into the timeless future. Do not be like the old me. For most of my marriage I failed to walk in love and be the firm foundation I should have been for my lovely wife and wonderful children. Self-absorbed with my own interests and wants, I turned a blind eye to the needs and desires of my closest neighbors, my family.

Prayer does not work when you refuse to humble yourself and obey the second great commandment, to love thy neighbor as thyself. Too many Christian men are deceived into thinking they can prosper in life without walking in love toward their wife and children. Jesus is not blind and cannot be fooled. He is the ultimate man and is the model for successful manhood.

NEHEMIAH: CALLING, EQUIPPING, AND OUTCOME

Calling (Builder):

> Then the king said to me, "What do you request?" So I prayed to the God of heaven. And I said to the king, "If it pleases the king, and if your servant has found favor in your sight, I ask that you send me to Judah, to the city of my fathers' tombs, that I may rebuild it." (Nehemiah 2:4–5 NKJV)

Equipping (Holy Spirit):

> And I told them of the hand of my God which had been good upon me, and also of the king's words that he had spoken to me. So they said, "Let us rise up and build." Then they set their hands to this good work. (Nehemiah 2:18 NKJV)

Outcome (Rebuilt Wall):

> So the wall was finished on the twenty-fifth day of Elul, in fifty-two days. (Nehemiah 6:15 NKJV)

WORSHIPER

To worship God is to obey God. Period. Worship can be manifested in diverse ways. Glorifying the Lord through song, dance, art, and other creative expressions are forms of worship. Acknowledging God through prayer, praise, and meditation are also examples of worship. Pleasing the Lord by loving, forgiving, and serving people are also forms of worship. God has called and equipped you to worship Him by obeying Him. Obedience brings success. Disobedience produces failure. God called you to win and not lose. It is up to you whether you prosper or suffer. Worship the Lord in Spirit and in truth. God is looking for people who will obey Him out of a pure heart and not a selfish spirit.

> To worship God is to obey God.

BACKGROUND: WHO WAS BEZALEL?

Now the LORD said to Moses, "See, I have called by name Bezalel, son of Uri, the son of Hur, of the tribe of Judah." (Exodus 31:1–2 AMP)

During the days of Moses, God called for a holy place to be built where priests could come and speak with Him. Man was tasked with building this place—known as a tabernacle or a sanctuary—and furnishing it with the altar of burnt offering, the mercy seat of God, and other important things. Sacrifices would be placed on the altar and incinerated. Sins would be brought to the mercy seat and forgiven.

Bezalel was an artisan called by God to prepare the sanctuary on earth where the priests would worship God. With sacrifices in hand, priests came before the Lord to seek forgiveness for their own sins and the sins of the people. This was often how priests worshiped God. Bezalel was a worshiper of the living God, but he was not a priest. He was not a praise and worship leader. He was a worshiper because he was obedient before God. When God called Bezalel, he responded. He did not hesitate, vacillate, or procrastinate. Bezalel acknowledged the call of God and went to work.

> I have filled him with the Spirit of God in wisdom and skill, in understanding and intelligence, in knowledge, and in all kinds of craftsmanship, to make artistic designs for work in gold, in silver, and in bronze, and in the cutting of stones for settings, and in the carving of wood, to work in all kinds of craftsmanship. (Exodus 31:3–5 AMP)

Bezalel was equipped with the Holy Spirit and power to do exactly what God called him to accomplish. The power he was given was the knowledge, wisdom, and understanding to make beautiful and useful things for the sanctuary of the Lord. Bezalel was not given the ability to go to war. He was not given the ability to work a farm. He was not given the ability to cast for fish. Bezalel was given the

> Bezalel was equipped with the Holy Spirit and power to do exactly what God called him to accomplish.

skills needed to build a physical place where priests would come and perform priestly duties.

God called Bezalel to build a sanctuary. It was Bezalel's choice to accept or reject the calling. Fortunately, he accepted. Although the grace of God may have permitted him to do something else for a season, he would have eventually failed. God does not give you grace to excuse you from doing what He created you to do. The purpose of the grace is to enable you to do what He called you to do. Disregarding the call of God on your life equates to trampling the grace of God under your feet. The blood of Jesus was spilled for you to be forgiven of your sins and live before God. What does living before God mean? Fulfilling your calling. Your calling is your purpose. Without a purpose, there is no reason to live.

> The purpose of the grace is to enable you to do what He called you to do.

> And behold, I Myself have appointed with him Oholiab, son of Ahisamach, of the tribe of Dan; to all who are wise-hearted I have given the skill and ability to make everything that I have commanded you. (Exodus 31:6 AMP)

God rarely—if ever—calls people to do things without anyone else being involved. Think about it. Adam had Eve. John the Baptist had disciples. Paul the Apostle had Barnabas. Even Jesus had a team of people around Him! God is three-in-one. He is Father, Son, and Holy Spirit. God Himself does not act alone, and neither should you. You were called into a community called mankind. It is a global network of living beings capable of great things. Tap into the greatest natural asset on earth: people. The return on investment is invaluable because God made people in His image and likeness. There is nothing more valuable on the planet than His creations that reflect His face.

Bezalel was not a one-man band. God appointed Oholiab to labor alongside him. Oholiab was also gifted and talented through the Holy Spirit to make everything God commanded to be made. Bezalel needed a team of people to carry out God's vision. Interestingly, Bezalel did not have to pick the team members. God recruited the people and gave them the skill to get the job done. How successful would your efforts be if you used this model? Let God select the people to help you complete the task He assigned. Bezalel did and made everything that God commanded Moses.

YOUR TASK

God gave you a job to do. Are you doing it? The very reason breath remains in your lungs is to complete a task—or set of tasks—on earth. Why were you selected to do a particular job? God knows, and He might share that information with you. However, you cannot wait until you receive a revelation on why you were selected before you act. Stand and walk where He told you to walk. Demonstrate great faith and proceed down the path you are to take.

> The very reason breath remains in your lungs is to complete a task—or set of tasks—on earth.

Do not sit around waiting for Jesus to appear and commission you to go forth. You do not need a personal appearance from the Prince of Peace to have "peace" about your task. You just need to accept your assignment and move forward.

YOUR TALENT

There is no skill or ability apart from God. The Lord made everything for a specific reason, including you. The knowledge you have to pick up a tool and make a priceless masterpiece is from the Lord. The wisdom you have to listen and render a good decision is from the Lord. The understanding you possess to assess challenges and develop sustainable solutions is from the Lord. You are a uniquely gifted and talented person. It is your decision as to whether you will invest yourself into the life you were destined to live. Every cell in your body was manufactured by the Creator of the universe. Every organ in your body was handcrafted by the Designer of the earth. Every pore in your skin was shaped by the Architect of the sun. Do not accept lies and deceptions from people who have no faith in the Lord. You are here to please God, not man.

> There is no skill or ability apart from God.

YOUR TEAM

Eve, the first woman, came from the rib of Adam, the first man. Every human being on earth descended from this first couple. Adam and Eve were a team. They were commanded to be fruitful, multiply, and subdue the earth. They were instructed to expand their team and conquer the world. If Adam and Eve did not need a team to fulfill their purpose, they would not have been told to grow their ranks. Teams are vital to success. They always have been and always will be important. Progress is made when multiple hands are engaged. Do not underestimate the power of the collective. Every part of your body must work together for you to function. Take that truth and apply it to each facet of your life. Multiply or die is a motto to live by.

BE DILIGENT

Diligence should be your precious possession. Bring the spirit of excellence with you wherever you go. It is in your divine nature to be productive and efficient. God does not waste anything and has a useful purpose for everything. The future is a product of either diligence or laziness. Diligence brings prosperity. Laziness brings poverty. It is your choice. Do not be fooled into thinking you can prosper without diligence or avoid poverty while being lazy. Choose what you want out of life.

> Strength amid a storm comes from a consistent, disciplined, and intentional lifestyle.

Strength amid a storm comes from a consistent, disciplined, and intentional lifestyle. Every Christian has the Holy Spirit dwelling inside. However, not every Christian is diligent. Fear, pride, selfishness, and other sins thrive when complacency abounds. There is a sweetness attached to planning and executing a plan. Confidence comes from undertaking a task and seeing it through to the end. Obedience is always better than sacrifice. Envision yourself pleasing God day-in and day-out. Although faith pleases God, faith without works is dead. The "works" needed to enliven our faith are actions of obedience. Obeying the Lord is worshiping the Lord. Grasp this truth and allow the Holy Spirit to minister the fullness of the understanding.

BEZALEL: CALLING, EQUIPPING, AND OUTCOME

Calling (Identified by Name):

Now the LORD said to Moses, "See, I have called by name Bezalel, son of Uri, the son of Hur, of the tribe of Judah." (Exodus 31:1–2 AMP)

Equipping (Spirit of God):

I have filled him with the Spirit of God in wisdom and skill, in understanding and intelligence, in knowledge, and in all kinds of craftsmanship, to make artistic designs for work in gold, in silver, and in bronze, and in the cutting of stones for settings, and in the carving of wood, to work in all kinds of craftsmanship. (Exodus 31:3–5 AMP)

Outcome (God's Tabernacle Built):

Now Bezalel the son of Uri, the son of Hur, of the tribe of Judah, made everything that the LORD commanded Moses. (Exodus 38:22 AMP)

SOWER

Sowers are called to plant seeds and reveal knowledge. They have a unique understanding of circumstances and a passion to share wisdom. Rarely content with being quiet amid ignorance, sowers are driven by a conviction to open eyes and turn people from darkness to light. They favor substance over form and fact over fiction. These purpose-driven people are intentional and results-oriented. Focused like a laser beam on planting the right seed, they have the strength and fortitude to endure hardship.

> Sowers are called to plant seeds and reveal knowledge.

BACKGROUND: WHO WAS PAUL THE APOSTLE?

> Paul, an apostle (not from men nor through man, but through Jesus Christ and God the Father who raised Him from the dead). (Galatians 1:1 NKJV)

Paul was an apostle, or special messenger, of God. Called to preach and teach the gospel of Jesus Christ before he was born, Paul was a devoted servant of the Lord. He was commissioned by God to spread truth and love to a beleaguered and hurt generation. Years of blindness and hypocrisy left many of his brethren jaded and broken. Not one to shrink from a challenge, Paul disrupted status quo mentality and preached Jesus Christ as the authentic Son of God.

Despised by the people he grew up and studied with, Paul walked without fear in proclaiming the resurrection power that raised Jesus from the dead. Christ was alive and well according to the gospel preached by Paul. Nothing on, beneath, or above earth could sway Paul into believing another truth. To this servant of the Lord, there was only one path to Father God: Jesus. Paul sowed this powerful truth wherever he went, and churches were launched as a result.

> But I make known to you, brethren, that the gospel which was preached by me is not according to man. For I neither received it from man, nor was I taught it, but it came through the revelation of Jesus Christ. (Galatians 1:11–12 NKJV)

Paul was crystal clear about the source of the gospel message he preached. The revelation about Jesus Christ crucified for the world was from God, not man. Telling the whole truth, and nothing but the truth, drove this strong man of God to declare and decree the sovereignty and sufficiency of Christ. His gospel message was not developed or deduced by a fallible man. It was determined and delivered by the infallible God. Paul was about purity and power and not about pride and pretense. Never satisfied with the gospel being labeled an evolution of human wisdom, he made clear wherever he went the wellspring of the truth. Heaven above and not the earth below was where the gospel originated. Like a good planter, he knew the source of his seed.

> For you have heard of my former conduct in Judaism,
> how I persecuted the church of God beyond measure
> and tried to destroy it. (Galatians 1:13 NKJV)

Once a brutal persecutor of Christians, Paul switched sides and believed in Christ after encountering Him enroute to Damascus. Engulfed in a bright light while on the road, he knew it was the Lord when he heard a voice speaking to him. Blinded for several days from the experience, Paul had time to reflect and think about his past behavior. Known as Saul of Tarsus prior to his conversion, he considered Christians enemies and dragged them out of their homes to be jailed. He even facilitated the stoning of Stephen, a devout and faithful man who loved the Lord and refused to compromise his beliefs.

Paul did his best to undermine and destroy the church. He was furious about some person named Jesus claiming to be the Son of God. Offended and disgusted, Paul spent years attacking believers and their beliefs. He was mean, harsh, and hardened. Anger and violence filled his heart. But why was he so unloving toward followers of the Lord? He was convinced the doctrine of Jesus Christ undermined the Law of Moses observed by his forefathers.

> And I advanced in Judaism beyond many of my contemporaries in my own nation, being more exceedingly zealous for the traditions of my fathers. (Galatians 1:14 NKJV)

Convinced that the gospel of Jesus Christ was blasphemous, Paul refused to believe in the message of salvation. Steeped in the Law of Moses from his youth, he was fervent in the doctrine of Judaism. Paul learned the Law from Gamaliel, the most revered Jewish teacher of the day. An "A" student who surpassed everyone in his generation, Paul became one of the leading experts on Judaism in the nation of Israel. In Paul's mind, the doctrine of Jesus Christ was incompatible to Jewish orthodoxy. He rejected the notion that salvation was possible apart from adherence to the Law of Moses. Paul thought anyone who believed Jesus was crucified for his or her sins and was raised from the dead was deluded. Faith in Christ produced nothing more than wicked people opposed to Father God, in his book.

> But when it pleased God, who separated me from my mother's womb and called me through His grace, to reveal His Son in me, that I might preach Him among the Gentiles, I did not immediately confer with flesh and blood. (Galatians 1:15–16 NKJV)

After conversion to Christ, Paul realized what he was called to do: preach the gospel. He also understood what he was called to be: an apostle. He was destined to sow seed and reveal Jesus Christ. It pleased God to separate Paul, as well as each one of us, from the womb to fulfill a special and unique purpose in the world. Fulfilling your calling in life pleases God because it takes faith in God to do what He has called you to do—and faith

> It pleased God to separate Paul, as well as each one of us, from the womb to fulfill a special and unique purpose in the world.

pleases God. Immersing yourself in the Word of God is a great way to build your faith since faith comes by hearing the Word. Be sure to build your faith upon a foundation of love, as faith works through love. Faith is crucial to walking out your purpose on earth. God deposited a measure of faith within you, which was His Holy Spirit. He is quite pleased when you are led by His Spirit and do what you were put on this planet to do.

> Who then is Paul, and who is Apollos, but ministers through whom you believed, as the Lord gave to each one? I planted, Apollos watered, but God gave the increase. (1 Corinthians 3:5–6 NKJV)

Paul was clear about his purpose. He knew he was a minister called to sow seed. The seed he sowed was the truth of the gospel of Jesus Christ. He was not afraid to deliver his message because he was confident that his message was true. Truth brings confidence, and confidence brings boldness. Boldness brings conviction, and conviction

> Paul was clear, convicted, and content about his calling as a sower.

brings contentment. True happiness in life is attained when peace abounds. Paul was clear, convicted, and content about his calling as a sower.

Through grace, Paul was equipped with the revelation of Jesus Christ—which is the Holy Spirit and the Holy Word of God—to prosper in his purpose. He preached the gospel and was used to convert many people to Christ. Never afraid to preach the Word of God with boldness, Paul made headway in his missionary outreach. What was the outcome?

Throngs of people glorified God as a previous Christian persecutor preached the faith he once tried to extinguish.

CLEAR

Clarity is a great word. It simply means seeing or knowing without obstruction. Paul discovered his calling after having an encounter with Jesus on the road to Damascus. When the bright light of Christ surrounded Him, he instantly knew it was the Lord speaking to him. After a period of personal reflection, Paul was clear about his calling to spread the gospel. Despite years and years of studying the Mosaic Law under the best teachers, Paul did not know why he was born until after Jesus spoke to him. The Word of God brings light to the darkness in believers' lives. Place yourself in the path of the Prince of Peace (Jesus Christ) by immersing yourself in His Word and being humble and obedient. His peace will illuminate the path you are to take in your heart. Be led not by the fear and anxiety spewing forth from the mouth of man. Be led by the love and truth flowing out of the mouth of God. The peace of God will bring all the clarity you need to succeed in life each and every day.

CONVICTED

To be convicted is to be convinced. Paul was convinced about the truth of the gospel of Jesus Christ. Nothing could move him away from it because he was rooted and grounded in the love of Christ. Love is the strongest force in the universe. God is love, and He made everything through Christ. You cannot outmaneuver, outthink, or outfox the Creator. Love is the secret to success in the kingdom of God. It powers faith, which enables you to do business with God.

Be convicted about Christ being your Lord and Savior. You cannot take off and fly without knowing the foundation upon which your soul stands. Jesus is the power and wisdom of God. Embracing such revelation by remaining focused on Christ at all times will keep you out of trouble. It will shield you from the storm and guard your heart during trials. Be like a tree planted by rivers of water (Psalm 1:3), and rest upon the peace of Christ.

CONTENT

Question: How can you experience joy amid pain?

<u>Answer</u>: Stay in the presence of God.

He is with you always. But are you with Him? He pledged to never leave you nor forsake you. But have you strayed away from Him? Pain comes to everyone at some point in their life. Whether it is physical, emotional, or spiritual, pain hits at some point in time. What do you do when it appears? Trust in God. You must master being content and happy regardless of the situation or circumstance.

For most people, that is an extremely hard thing to do. I have often found myself struggling to remain content during a crisis. Though I have fallen short many times, I do realize the importance of being close to God. True joy and happiness is the will of God for each and every person on earth. Experience what He desires you to have all the time. Decide to follow the Lord and Savior of the world, and contentment will be your close companion.

BE COMMITTED

Sowers are specialists designed to perform special tasks at specific times. Precise and purposeful in their actions, they invest themselves into planting seeds for future harvests. Sowers are not tentative and temporary. They are strategic and long-term. Their thoughts, words, and actions line up with their assignment. Sowers are committed to completing their job, even if they do not see results with their own eyes.

What is your level of commitment to fulfilling your purpose? Are you all-in or tip-toeing around the periphery? Be decisive, and dedi-

cate yourself to realizing your fullest potential in Christ Jesus. Give all
you have to be all you can be in Christ.
Doing so will give glory and honor to
God, and He honors those who honor
Him. Do not hold yourself back.

> Give all you have to be all you can be in Christ.

Release yourself into His hand and find yourself inside His plan. In
Him, you will find your place and possess your peace.

If you are still in the process of self-discovery, stay the course and
do not become anxious. Demonstrate to God your passion for serving
Him and people. He will reward you with one of the greatest gifts
He gives to man: wisdom. He will reveal His will for your life and
steer you toward your promised land through His wisdom. He takes
pleasure in the success of His children. Allow the Lord to prosper you
by allowing Him to lead you.

Commit yourself to the Lord, and you will see His commitment
to you. I am not saying He will commit to you after you commit to
Him. Rather, I am saying you will *see* His commitment to you after
you commit to Him. The best vision is not 20/20 vision with human
eyes but 3/1 vision with spiritual eyes. When you see the Father, Son,
and Spirit (3) as one (1) unified divine being dwelling within you, and
you commit to following Him, your spiritual eyes will be opened. You
will see His amazing commitment to you in the spirit realm. It will
be more real to you than the face you see in the mirror. Commit—or
recommit—yourself to God today!

PAUL THE APOSTLE: CALLING, EQUIPPING, AND OUTCOME

Calling (Reveal Christ):

> But when it pleased God, who separated me from my mother's womb and called me through His grace, to reveal His Son in me, that I might preach Him among the Gentiles, I did not immediately confer with flesh and blood, nor did I go up to Jerusalem to those who were apostles before me; but I went to Arabia, and returned again to Damascus. (Galatians 1:15–17 NKJV)

Equipping (Revelation of Christ):

> But I make known to you, brethren, that the gospel which was preached by me is not according to man. For I neither received it from man, nor was I taught it, but it came through the revelation of Jesus Christ. (Galatians 1:11–12 NKJV)

Outcome (God Glorified):

> And I was unknown by face to the churches of Judea which were in Christ. But they were hearing only, "He who formerly persecuted us now preaches the faith which he once tried to destroy." And they glorified God in me. (Galatians 1:22–24 NKJV)

YOUR MOVE

WALK IN LOVE

Walking in love toward God and man is the master key to realizing your calling, equipping, and outcomes potential in Christ Jesus. You cannot find and fulfill the reason for the breath of God within your lungs without surrendering yourself to Him. As noted in the introduction to this book, to surrender means to accept Jesus Christ as both *Savior* and *Lord*. Walking in love is the evidence that you have accepted Jesus Christ. Acknowledge that the blood of Jesus paid the ransom for your sin and secured your forgiveness. Recognize that Father God raised His only Son Jesus Christ from the dead and welcomed you into the fellowship of believers. Receive the empowerment of the Holy Spirit and be led by the Holy Spirit.

There is no substitute for genuine and sincere love. Everyone who desires to live with God for eternity is called to love Him and give their life to Him. This is the model presented to us in John 3:16. God loved the world so much that He gave what was most precious—the life of His Son Jesus Christ. Do not underestimate the power of love. Love makes faith work, and faith enables you to please God. Do not undervalue the necessity of love. Without love you are nothing, can be nothing, and will have nothing. This is because God is love, and without God you are nothing, can be nothing, and will have nothing. Love is the preeminent virtue.

> Though I speak with the tongues of men and of angels, but have not love, I have become sounding brass or a clanging cymbal. And though I have the gift of prophecy, and understand all mysteries and all knowledge, and though I have all faith, so that I could remove mountains, but have not love, I am nothing. And though I bestow all my goods to feed the poor, and though I give my body to be burned, but have not love, it profits me nothing. Love suffers long and is kind; love does not envy; love does not parade itself, is not puffed up; does not behave rudely, does not seek its own, is not provoked, thinks no evil; does not rejoice in iniquity, but rejoices in the truth; bears all things, believes all things, hopes all things, endures all things. Love never fails. But whether there are prophecies, they will fail; whether there are tongues, they will cease; whether there is knowledge, it will vanish away. For we know in part and we prophesy in part. But when that which is perfect has come, then that which is in part will be done away. When I was a child, I spoke as a child, I understood as a child, I thought as a child; but when I became a man, I put away childish things. For now we see in a mirror, dimly, but then face to face. Now I know in part, but then I shall

know just as I also am known. And now abide faith, hope, love, these three; but the greatest of these is love. (1 Corinthians 13 NKJV)

OBEY GOD AND LIVE

To love God is to obey God. There is no skirting this hard truth. We must learn to embrace this unavoidable reality and live it each and every day. The consequence of not grasping this concept and walking it out daily is unpleasant. Eve did not love God, and one day disobeyed. For that choice she lost her life, and Adam lost his. Failing to obey God is tantamount to losing the will to live. Regardless of what reward or pleasure you think you might receive from turning your back on the one who created you, it is not worth it. Do not chase after false gold and falter before the true God.

Live to realize your calling, equipping, and outcomes potential in Christ Jesus by obeying God. Success and failure are determined by whether you obey or disobey. Without obeying God, you cannot fulfill His will. Moreover, you may very well lose your God-given appointment or position. Adam and Eve forfeited their rulership over the earth because they disobeyed God. A similar fate befell Saul who lost his kingship over Israel due to disobedience. Consider a few passages:

> Live to realize your calling, equipping, and outcomes potential in Christ Jesus by obeying God.

Then Samuel said to Saul, "Be quiet! And I will tell

215

you what the Lord said to me last night." And he said to him, "Speak on." So Samuel said, "When you were little in your own eyes, were you not head of the tribes of Israel? And did not the Lord anoint you king over Israel? "Now the Lord sent you on a mission, and said, 'Go, and utterly destroy the sinners, the Amalekites, and fight against them until they are consumed.' Why then did you not obey the voice of the Lord? Why did you swoop down on the spoil, and do evil in the sight of the Lord?" (1 Samuel 15:16–19 NKJV)

And Saul said to Samuel, "But I have obeyed the voice of the Lord, and gone on the mission on which the Lord sent me, and brought back Agag king of Amalek; I have utterly destroyed the Amalekites. But the people took of the plunder, sheep and oxen, the best of the things which should have been utterly destroyed, to sacrifice to the Lord your God in Gilgal." (1 Samuel 15:20–21 NKJV)

So Samuel said: "Has the Lord as great delight in burnt offerings and sacrifices, As in obeying the voice of the Lord? Behold, to obey is better than sacrifice, And to heed than the fat of rams. For rebellion is as the sin of witchcraft, And stubbornness is as iniquity and idolatry. Because you have rejected the word of

the LORD, He also has rejected you from being king."
(Samuel 15:22–23 NKJV)

Then Saul said to Samuel, "I have sinned, for I have transgressed the commandment of the LORD and your words, because I feared the people and obeyed their voice. Now therefore, please pardon my sin, and return with me, that I may worship the LORD." But Samuel said to Saul, "I will not return with you, for you have rejected the word of the LORD, and the LORD has rejected you from being king over Israel." (1 Samuel 15:24–26 NKJV)

Though God anointed Saul to be king over Israel and set him up to succeed, Saul failed because he rejected the word of the Lord. God rejected him as king over Israel because of his actions. Saul's foolishness disqualified him from continuing in his God-given position. You cannot reject God's authority and expect to succeed. Failure will be imminent. The only recourse is to admit wrongdoing and ask for mercy. God will act upon your request when you approach Him in faith, with a humble and obedient heart. He hears the prayers of the righteous but closes His ears to the voice of the unfaithful, prideful, and disobedient. Live to testify about God fulfilling your calling.

> Though God anointed Saul to be king over Israel and set him up to succeed, Saul failed because he rejected the word of the Lord.

DISOBEY GOD AND DIE

Disobey God, and your dreams shall die. Persist in your sin, and you may lose your life. Christians who disobey God are walking in pride and playing with hellfire. While obedience is the key to life, disobedience is the door to death. God gave you the power to turn the key or open the door. The choice is yours. Noah obeyed God and lived. Adam and Eve disobeyed God and died.

> Disobey God, and your dreams shall die.

And to Adam He said, Because you have listened and given heed to the voice of your wife and have eaten of the tree of which I commanded you, saying, You shall not eat of it, the ground is under a curse because of you; in sorrow and toil shall you eat [of the fruits] of it all the days of your life. Thorns also and thistles shall it bring forth for you, and you shall eat the plants of the field. In the sweat of your face shall you eat bread until you return to the ground, for out of it you were taken; for dust you are and to dust you shall return. The man called his wife's name Eve [life spring], because she was the mother of all the living. (Genesis 3:17–20 AMPC)

For Adam also and for his wife the Lord God made long coats [tunics] of skins and clothed them. And the Lord God said, Behold, the man has become like one of Us [the Father, Son, and Holy Spirit], to know [how to distinguish between] good and evil and blessing and calamity; and now, lest he put forth his hand and take also from the tree of life and eat, and live forever—Therefore the Lord God sent him forth from the Garden of Eden to till the ground from which he was taken. So [God] drove out the man; and He placed at the east of the Garden of Eden the cherubim and a flaming sword which turned every way, to keep and guard the way to the tree of life. (Genesis 3:21–24 AMPC)

Adam and Eve's calling to conquer the earth and everything in it died when they obeyed Satan. Their opportunity to have endless life on earth died when they were expelled from the garden of Eden. They experienced physical death after a lifetime of struggle. The tree of life, which would have enabled them to live forever, was at their disposal—but they lost the right to eat from it after violating God's command and eating fruit from the tree of the knowledge of good and evil. They failed to fulfill their calling because they chose to walk the path of sin and shame. Do not follow in their footsteps.

SIN NO MORE

Disobedience is sin, and you can live without it. God designed you to walk in love and not walk in sin. Yes, you

Disobedience is sin, and you can live without it.

were born in sin, but you do not need to die in sin. Put another way, although you were born a failure, you do not need to die a failure. The will of God is for you to walk with Him. There is no law requiring you to live in sin. Jesus died in your place so you would not need to die for your sins. He was without sin and gave us the power over sin. There is no excuse for committing sin. How you were born is not how you need to die. Sin is a choice. God wants you to choose wisely. Die to sin and awake to righteousness. Follow in the footsteps of Christ, who is our example.

> For to this you were called, because Christ also suffered for us, leaving us an example, that you should follow His steps: "Who committed no sin, Nor was deceit found in his mouth"; who, when He was reviled, did not revile in return; when He suffered, He did not threaten, but committed Himself to Him who judges righteously; who Himself bore our sins in His own body on the tree, that we, having died to sins, might live for righteousness—by whose stripes you were healed. (1 Peter 2:21–24 NKJV)

Is it possible to live a life without sin? Is it possible to refrain from evil thoughts, words, and deeds every day? Is it possible to be perfect before God always? Yes, it is. God does not want you to be a slave of sin. He called you to be free from it. We know this is true from the words Jesus spoke after he healed a sick man and forgave an adulteress:

Sick Man:

> But the one who was healed did not know who it was, for Jesus had withdrawn, a multitude being in that place. Afterward Jesus found him in the temple, and said to him, "See, you have been made well. Sin no more, lest a worse thing come upon you." The man departed and told the Jews that it was Jesus who had made him well. (John 5:13–15 NKJV)

Adulteress:

> When Jesus had raised Himself up and saw no one but the woman, He said to her, "Woman, where are those accusers of yours? Has no one condemned you?" She said, "No one, Lord." And Jesus said to her, "Neither do I condemn you; go and sin no more." Then Jesus spoke to them again, saying, "I am the light of the world. He who follows Me shall not walk in darkness, but have the light of life." (John 8:10–12 NKJV)

JESUS SAID, "SIN NO MORE"

In both instances, Jesus told the person to "sin no more." Jesus wouldn't have said "sin no more" unless they were capable of not sinning anymore. Otherwise, Jesus would have been lying

> Jesus wouldn't have said "sin no more" unless they were capable of not sinning anymore.

when He said, "sin no more." Keep in mind these were two Jewish people living under the old covenant Law of Moses sealed by the blood of animals and not under the new covenant grace of Christ sealed by the blood of Jesus. Faith in God, even prior to the blood of Jesus being shed, was sufficient to empower someone to live sin free. The sick man testified to others that Jesus healed him. The adulteress confessed to Christ that He was Lord. The man and the woman both had hearts committed to Christ. They were ready to receive instructions to live without sin because they could obey instructions to live without sin. Jesus will not tell you to do something you are incapable of doing. To do so would be unfair, unjust, and ungodly. Christ cannot be something He is not. Why should you?

WHAT ABOUT KING SOLOMON'S WORDS?

For there is not a just man on earth who does good and does not sin. (Ecclesiastes 7:20 NKJV)

The Old Testament book of Ecclesiastes is traditionally attributed to King Solomon, who was the son of King David and ruled over Israel. It's widely believed King Solomon wrote Ecclesiastes toward the end of his life. It highlights wisdom from one of the wisest kings to have ever walked upon the face of the earth. This raises an intriguing—but uncomfortable—question: If King Solomon, who was given great wisdom from God to rule Israel, said there is no righteous man on earth who does good and does not sin, then how can someone live without sin? Obedience is the obvious, and only, answer to this question. Being just and righteous before God does not exempt you from sin. However, it enables you to access the power that conquered sin, the Spirit of Christ. Through Jesus Christ you can be sin-free. Despite God's wisdom resident within his heart, King Solomon disobeyed God: he had intimate relations with multiple women and turned his heart from God. This behavior stained his otherwise excellent record.

> Being just and righteous before God does not exempt you from sin.

> But King Solomon loved many foreign women, as well as the daughter of Pharaoh: women of the Moabites, Ammonites, Edomites, Sidonians, and Hittites—from the nations of whom the LORD had said to the children of Israel, "You shall not intermarry with them, nor they with you. Surely they will turn away your hearts after their gods." Solomon clung to these in love. And he had seven hundred wives, princesses, and three hundred concubines; and his wives turned away his heart. For it was so, when Solomon was old, that his wives turned his heart after other gods; and his heart was not loyal to the LORD his God, as was the heart of his father David. (1 Kings 11:1–4 NKJV)

Decide Today: Accept what Christ has commanded you to do: to love. Love God and love your neighbor as yourself. Love will bring health to your flesh. Love will bring wealth to your world. Love will drive fear out of your life. Love will cure your sickness of sin. Anyone who tells you a person cannot live without sin is a liar because they are saying you cannot live in love. Jesus told the disbelieving and loveless Pharisees they were of their father the devil. Do not be a child of Satan, who is the father of lies. He wants you to believe a lifestyle of sin is acceptable and a lifestyle of love is impossible. Do not be confused by the master of confusion who seeks your soul and desires your demise. Remember, deception is the tool of the devil to defeat and destroy you. Do not forget you already have victory over Satan through the blood of Jesus and the words of your testimony. Declare and decree Jesus is Lord and Savior each and every day. Your words shape your world. Live in freedom.

OBEY THE COMMANDMENT OF LOVE

The love commandment is the principal commandment. Loving the Lord and your neighbor are two sides of the same love coin. God is love and everything in the spirit and natural realms revolve around Him. The entire Word of God stands upon the foundation of love and the Holy Spirit of God works through love. The Bible tells of great men and women who succeeded because they loved God and their neighbor. Abraham battled armies on behalf of his beloved nephew, Lot, and won because God was with him. Later Abraham put God first in his life when he did not withhold his son of promise, Isaac, from the Lord. Joseph was another prime example of a person who loved God. He refused to compromise his walk with God when Potiphar's wife tempted him. Joseph forgave

> The Bible tells of great men and women who succeeded because they loved God and their neighbor.

his brothers for selling him into slavery because he knew God sent him to Egypt to deliver his people.

Abraham and Joseph loved those who dwelt with them. They epitomized loving your neighbor as yourself. You cannot expect to go very far with God without walking in love toward man, who was created after His likeness and image. People are important to God, which means they should be important to you too. Anything less than a total attitude of love is selfish and falls short of the glory of God (Romans 3:23). I know about this because I dwelt in the dungeon of deception for decades. I thought I was more important than others and treated people poorly. Although I achieved a level of professional success, I descended to the realm of personal failure. God opened my eyes to see the wickedness in my heart, the corruption in my mind, and the taint on my soul. I repented from my sin and recommitted myself to Jesus Christ. I did not want to be a member of the loveless church.

> To the angel (messenger) of the assembly (church) in
> Ephesus write: These are the words of Him Who holds
> the seven stars [which are the messengers of the seven
> churches] in His right hand, Who goes about among
> the seven golden lampstands [which are the seven
> churches]: I know your industry and activities, labori-
> ous toil and trouble, and your patient endurance, and
> how you cannot tolerate wicked [men] and have tested
> and critically appraised those who call [themselves]
> apostles (special messengers of Christ) and yet are not,
> and have found them to be impostors and liars. I know
> you are enduring patiently and are bearing up for My

name's sake, and you have not fainted or become exhausted or grown weary. But I have this [one charge to make] against you: that you have left (abandoned) the love that you had at first [you have deserted Me, your first love]. Remember then from what heights you have fallen. Repent (change the inner man to meet God's will) and do the works you did previously [when first you knew the Lord], or else I will visit you and remove your lampstand from its place, unless you change your mind and repent. (Revelation 2:1–5 AMPC)

GOD'S TIMING

To everything there is a season, and a time for every matter or purpose under heaven: A time to be born and a time to die, a time to plant and a time to pluck up what is planted, A time to kill and a time to heal, a time to break down and a time to build up, A time to weep and a time to laugh, a time to mourn and a time to dance, A time to cast away stones and a time to gather stones together, a time to embrace and a time to refrain from embracing, A time to get and a time to lose, a time to keep and a time to cast away, A time to rend and a time to sew, a time to keep silence and a time to speak, A time to love and a time to hate, a time for war and a time for peace. (Ecclesiastes 3:1–8 AMPC)

What does God want you to do during these times? What does God want you to do this year? What does God want you to do this month? What does God want you to do this week? What does God want you to do this day? What does God want you to do this hour? What does God want you to do this minute? What does God want you to do this second? What does God want you to do this moment? What does God want you to do right now?

There is a specific time for everything to happen. You were born into this natural world on a particular day and at a specific time. There was no accident, mishap, or mistake. You were separated from your mother's womb when it needed to happen. God is intentional, purposeful, and faithful.

> There is a specific time for everything to happen.

He called you to live and breathe in this day and age to play a special role and complete a unique work. Billions upon billions of people have walked the planet earth since the days of Adam and Eve. However, you are the one and only you to have ever lived. Believe it or not, you are living during the time you were supposed to live in. Respect the days of your life, which are limited. Time is your greatest resource and is worth more than money. Think about it. Lost time costs far more than lost money. You can regenerate a dollar but you cannot regenerate a minute. Value your time more than you value your money.

What are you going to do with the power He gave you? What are you going to do with the authority He gave you? What are you going to do with the name He gave you? What are you going to do with the wealth He gave you? What are you going to do with the body He gave you? What are you going to do with the mind He gave you? What are you going to do with the relationships He gave you? What are you going to do with the opportunities He gave you? What are you going to do with the breath of life He gave you?

God planted His Son Jesus Christ into Mary's womb at a specific time. His divine plan for the redemption of the human race unfolded in a carefully choreographed and orchestrated manner. Jesus was empowered with the Holy Spirit to succeed and faithfully carried out His calling. He was tortured and tormented upon the cross to enable everyone who calls on His name to access the same Holy Spirit. The power of God raised Jesus from the dead and dwells in us and empowers us to succeed, just like Christ.

God did not give you great things for no apparent reason. You were designed to be more than a carbon footprint on the earth He created. Diverse resources were granted to you at birth and added after you were born. Invest your time, talent, and treasure into people. You will realize the greatest return possible when you add value to another person's life. This divine investment strategy is modeled after God. He invested in every person on earth when He sowed Jesus Christ into the world. God reaped a family of children because of His actions. What you sow is what you reap. The law of sowing and reaping is applicable to everyone, regardless of whether they know Jesus Christ or not.

> While the earth remains, seedtime and harvest, cold and heat, summer and winter, and day and night shall not cease. (Genesis 8:22 AMPC)

YOUR TIME IS NOW!

For He says, In the time of favor (of an assured welcome) I have listened to and heeded your call, and I
have helped you on the day of deliverance (the day of
salvation). Behold, now is truly the time for a gracious
welcome and acceptance [of you from God]; behold,
now is the day of salvation! (2 Corinthians 6:2 AMPC)

Today, God has called you to be righteous and not unrighteous.
Sin separates us from God. He wants us to draw close to Him.
Fortunately, our sin does not separate us from His love. He loved us
while we were yet sinners. However, we
will not be permitted to dwell with
Him forever if we insist on living in sin.
Friend, please do not allow the truth

> Today, God has called
> you to be righteous and
> not unrighteous.

outlined here to cause you to walk in guilt and condemnation. Our
flesh is weak and the Lord knows it. This is why He said He will forgive us if we confess our sins. Do not procrastinate and delay. Admit
your wrongdoing today. Tomorrow is not promised to anyone.

If we say we have no sin [refusing to admit that we are
sinners], we delude and lead ourselves astray, and the
Truth [which the Gospel presents] is not in us [does
not dwell in our hearts]. If we [freely] admit that we
have sinned and confess our sins, He is faithful and just
(true to His own nature and promises) and will forgive

our sins [dismiss our lawlessness] and [continuously] cleanse us from all unrighteousness [everything not in conformity to His will in purpose, thought and action]. If we say (claim) we have not sinned, we contradict His Word and make him out to be false and a liar, and His Word is not in us [the divine message of the Gospel is not in our hearts]. (1 John 1:8–10 AMPC)

Today, walk in love. Nothing cures sin and shame better than love. The best antidote for every sickness and disease is love. The soundest response to every calamity and catastrophe known to man is love. It is within the capacity of every human being to show love and restraint during the midst of troubles, trials and tribulations. The test of faith is the proving ground of love. Is your love strong enough to withstand persistent attacks and relentless assaults from the enemy? Will you crack under pressure and respond in anger and arrogance when your buttons are pressed? Can you remain calm and cool when the heat turns up and you begin to sweat? The level of love within your heart will govern your reactions to unpleasant, unfair, and unreal situations. Master love and master your life. Everything must be done in the spirit of love.

> Nothing cures sin and shame better than love.

Let all that you do be done with love.

(1 Corinthians 16:14 NKJV)

LESSONS FROM LEADERS

> For in Christ Jesus neither circumcision nor uncir-
> cumcision avails anything, but faith working through
> love. (Galatians 5:6 NKJV)

What do all the biblical leaders profiled in this book have in common? They exhibited love. Whether it was toward God, man, or both,
they walked in faith—and faith works through love. No move of faith
can occur apart from love. God is love and the Holy Spirit is faith.
Faith working through love means the Holy Spirit works through
God. Grasp this truth, and your life will change. The breath of life
within your lungs is a measure of the Holy Spirit of God placed within
you by God. It makes complete sense that the Holy Spirit of God does
not—and cannot—operate separate and distinct from God. The Holy
Spirit does not operate on its own authority. It does and speaks the
will of God. There is no distance between God and His Holy Spirit.
Walk in love, and you will walk by faith. This is a powerful truth.
Freedom from sin is found here. Walking in love enables you to walk
in the Holy Spirit, which in turn protects you from succumbing to the
lust of the flesh.

> But I say, walk and live [habitually] in the [Holy] Spirit
> [responsive to and controlled and guided by the Spirit];
> then you will certainly not gratify the cravings and
> desires of the flesh (of human nature without God).
> For the desires of the flesh are opposed to the [Holy]
> Spirit, and the [desires of the] Spirit are opposed to

the flesh (godless human nature); for these are antagonistic to each other [continually withstanding and in conflict with each other], so that you are not free but are prevented from doing what you desire to do. But if you are guided (led) by the [Holy] Spirit, you are not subject to the Law. (Galatians 5:16–18 AMPC)

The heroes of faith written about in the Bible walked in the Spirit. They were not moved by what their eyes saw or ears heard. Inputs received and processed by their natural senses did not order their footsteps. Rather, their destiny was determined by knowledge and wisdom acquired through spiritual discernment. Trusting God was essential to each person's success. They followed dictates from heaven and not deceptions from hell. Repeatedly tested and tried, these mortal people rejected man's wisdom and grasped God's power. They obeyed God, walked in humility, and often experienced miracles. Their lives are testimonies about the grace, goodness, and greatness of God.

> The heroes of faith written about in the Bible walked in the Spirit.

God has prepared a path for everyone to follow. The question is whether you are committed to doing what it takes to move forward. The heroes of faith decided to walk in the Spirit—they walked by faith. God moved in each of their lives in wondrous ways as a result of their faith working through love.

Scriptures casting a spotlight upon their faith, favor, humility, or obedience are below.

Noah:

And Noah did according to all that the LORD commanded him. (Genesis 7:5 NKJV)

Joseph:

Then Pharaoh said to Joseph, "Inasmuch as God has shown you all this, there is no one as discerning and wise as you. You shall be over my house, and all my people shall be ruled according to your word; only in regard to the throne will I be greater than you." (Genesis 41:39–40 NKJV)

Joshua:

The LORD said to Moses, "Take Joshua the son of Nun, a man in whom is the Spirit, and lay your hand on him; and have him stand before Eleazar the priest and before the whole congregation, and give him a commission in their sight." (Numbers 27:18–19 AMP)

Ezekiel:

So I prophesied as I was commanded; and as I prophesied, there was a noise, and suddenly a rattling; and the bones came together, bone to bone. (Ezekiel 37:7 NKJV)

David:

Then Samuel took the horn of oil and anointed David in the presence of his brothers; and the Spirit of the LORD came mightily upon David from that day forward. And Samuel arose and went to Ramah. (1 Samuel 16:13 AMP)

John the Baptist:

"For he will be great in the sight of the Lord, and shall drink neither wine nor strong drink. He will also be filled with the Holy Spirit, even from his mother's womb. And he will turn many of the children of Israel to the Lord their God." (Luke 1:15–16 NKJV)

Nehemiah:

And I told them of the hand of my God which had been good upon me, and also of the king's words that he had spoken to me. So they said, "Let us rise up and build." Then they set their hands to this good work. (Nehemiah 2:18 NKJV)

Bezalel:

Bezalel the son of Uri, the son of Hur, of the tribe of Judah, made all that the LORD had commanded Moses. (Exodus 38:22 NKJV)

Paul the Apostle:

> This man heard Paul speaking. Paul, observing him intently and seeing that he had faith to be healed, said with a loud voice, "Stand up straight on your feet!" And he leaped and walked. (Acts 14:9–10 NKJV)

RECONCILE YOUR FUTURE, PRESENT, AND PAST

Establish the right relationship between your future, present, and past. Doing so will enable you to better understand who you will be, who you are, and who you were. Putting these three life dimensions in the proper spiritual context will reveal important insights into your heart. Out of your heart will flow thoughts, words, and deeds. The central processing unit you possess is your heart. Like a computer, the heart needs maintenance. Ask yourself the following three questions to understand and diagnose your heart:

1. Future: What is the best vision of your future?

2. Present: What must you do today to realize the future vision?

3. Past: What can you learn from the past to inform what you should do today?

Love should be the common denominator between your future, present, and past. Does your best future vision involve love? Do your actions today reflect love? Do your past actions involve love? Carefully consider these probing questions, and fully embrace *your* truth. Running from *your* truth will move you backward. Be a person of love, and move forward. If you find yourself with a love deficit, ask God for help. Be quiet, listen, and obey. God is love and will show you how to succeed tomorrow, prosper today, and overcome yesterday. Love reveals your reality. Where you see love, you will see light and hope. Where you do not see love, you will see darkness and despair. Love determines the condition of your heart. If love is consistently evident in your thoughts, words, and deeds, your heart will be healthy. If love is far from you, your heart will be unhealthy.

> Love reveals your reality.

Structure your plans around walking in love toward God and man. Whatever you do should glorify God and bless people. That does not necessarily mean you are supposed to be in a pulpit preaching. It means you should pursue fulfilling your God-given calling in Christ Jesus and adding value to others. Do not live a selfish and isolated life. Doing what God called you to do will require walking in faith and love. This lifestyle brings glory to God. Fulfilling your divine calling will result in other people being blessed. You may not even need to say anything to anyone. People observing and watching your love-filled life will see the glory of God upon you and be inspired to live in like manner. Walking in love draws the favor of God like a magnet attracts a nail. People will be blessed by emulating your faithful lifestyle.

> Walking in love draws the favor of God like a magnet attracts a nail.

FINAL THOUGHTS

God displayed His love for the world by giving it the most valuable thing to Him: Jesus. As God's creation, we should follow suit. Love God and give Him what matters the most to you: your life. Accept Jesus Christ today as your Lord and Savior. Call on the name of the Lord, and you shall be saved (Romans 10:13). Ask for forgiveness for your sins, and you shall be forgiven.

> But what does it say? "The word is near you, in your mouth and in your heart" (that is, the word of faith which we preach): that if you confess with your mouth the Lord Jesus and believe in your heart that God has raised Him from the dead, you will be saved. For with the heart one believes unto righteousness, and with the mouth confession is made unto salvation. For the Scripture says, "Whoever believes on Him will not be put to shame." (Romans 10:8–11 NKJV)

Be motivated by love in everything you do, and the Lord will back you up. Love powers faith, and faith is required to please God. Nothing you think, say, or do will have any enduring value without love. Love is the necessary ingredient for success, peace, and prosperity. When you walk in love toward God and man, you will find and fulfill your God-given calling. Regardless of whether God called you to comfort, deliver, conquer, watch, inspire, challenge, build, worship, or sow, you need love in order to run your race and win. Great leaders from the Bible profiled in this book all shared the most important

Great leaders from the Bible profiled in this book all shared the most important dynamic in life: love.

dynamic in life: love. Love enabled their faith to work, and they demonstrated love through obedience. To love God is to obey God. You will realize your calling, equipping, and outcomes potential in Christ Jesus by obeying the Holy Word and Holy Spirit of God. Master obedience with a humble heart, and you will see God move with power and might in your life. Love people, and the love of God will remain with you.

> Beloved, if God loved us so [very much], we also ought to love one another. No man has at any time [yet] seen God. But if we love one another, God abides (lives and remains) in us and His love (that love which is essentially His) is brought to completion (to its full maturity, runs its full course, is perfected) in us! (1 John 4:11–12 AMPC)

PRAYER OF SALVATION

Father God, I confess with my mouth and believe in my heart that Jesus Christ is your only Son, that He died for my sins, and was raised from the dead by Your hand. I am a sinner and ask that you forgive me for my sins. Thank you, Father God, for forgiveness and salvation in the name of my Lord and Savior, Jesus Christ! Amen!

KAMAL I. LATHAM

An accomplished executive, diplomat, entrepreneur, and financial analyst, Kamal has facilitated over $5 billion in economic growth. He has lived and worked in major global business centers such as New York, Paris and Beijing. Kamal earned a Bachelor of Arts degree from Temple University and a Master in Public Policy degree from the Kennedy School of Government at Harvard University. You can follow Kamal at www.KamalLatham.com.

NOTES

NOTES

NOTES

NOTES

NOTES

NOTES

NOTES

NOTES

NOTES

NOTES

NOTES

NOTES

NOTES

NOTES

NOTES

NOTES

NOTES

NOTES

CPSIA information can be obtained
at www.ICGtesting.com
Printed in the USA
LVHW031543260321
682584LV00025B/495/J